I0090050

Relationship
INTENSIVE CARE

Relationship
INTENSIVE CARE

A PRACTICAL GUIDE TO SAVING AND MAINTAINING YOUR RELATIONSHIP

Leonie Ruth Schilling

Disclaimer

This guide is not intended for use by couples struggling with substance abuse, compulsive disorders such as gambling or domestic violence issues. All the information, techniques, skills and concepts contained within this publication are of the nature of general comment only and are not in any way recommended as individual advice. The intent is to offer a variety of information to provide a wider range of choices now and in the future, recognising that we all have widely diverse circumstances and viewpoints. Should any reader choose to make use of the information contained herein, this is their decision, and the author and publishers do not assume any responsibilities whatsoever under any condition or circumstances. It is recommended that the reader obtain their own independent advice.

First Edition 2016

Copyright © 2016 by Leonie Ruth Schilling

All rights reserved. No part of this publication may be reproduced, stored in a retrieval system, or transmitted in any form or by any means, electronic, mechanical, photocopying, recording or otherwise, without the prior written permission from the author.

National Library of Australia Cataloguing-in-Publication entry

Creator: Schilling, Leonie Ruth, author.

Title: Relationship Intensive Care: / A practical guide to saving and maintaining your relationship / Leonie Ruth Schilling.

ISBN: 9781925471007 (paperback)

Subjects:
Interpersonal relations.
Man-woman relationships
Interpersonal communication.

Dewey Number: 306.7

Copies of this book, work sheets and contracts can be obtained by visiting www.northlakescounsellingservices.com.au

Graphic Design & illustration by NGirl Design. www.ngirldesign.com.au

Published by Author Express
publish@authorexpress.com
www.AuthorExpress.com

Dedication

I dedicate this book with love
to my children
Candice and Dustin

Relationship
INTENSIVE CARE

A PRACTICAL GUIDE TO SAVING AND MAINTAINING YOUR RELATIONSHIP

COPIES OF THIS BOOK, WORK SHEETS AND
CONTRACTS CAN BE OBTAINED BY VISITING

www.northlakescounsellingservices.com.au

You can also book one on one sessions with Leonie
Schilling by visiting the above web address or calling
Ph: 07 3886 2715 or M: 0423 653 841.

Contents

Preface

After over thirty years working in hospitals and schools, I founded my counselling practice in 2007 and slowly built my reputation as a no-nonsense counsellor who uses a solution-focused, strength-based approach to help clients address their issues. Around the same time, I started to write a weekly column in a popular magazine. As people got to know me and my approach, my counselling practice not only grew but thrived. I listened to people talk about their relationships and always wondered why they're so disposable, with divorces easy to get and subsequent relationships that also tended to fail. Conversely, I wondered why in the world people stayed in clearly dysfunctional, and even abusive, relationships.

Over the years as I worked with couples, I noticed a common theme. Many were in their second, third or fourth long-term relationship or marriage and were once again having the same issues. It was obvious to me that people would leave one relationship thinking their partner was the problem or that they were incompatible, and then take their learned dysfunctional behaviours into the next relationship with no lessons learned. This would again result in an unsuccessful union. Like a bad movie playing out time and again. You could write the script of what the arguments would be about, what the patterns of discontent would be and how the relationship would wind up being undermined, just like the relationship that came before.

Another constant has been the breakup-and-get-back-together cycle. This is the couple most of you know who keep breaking up and getting back together time and time again. The true madness in this scenario is they get back together without a plan to change the issues that have been driving the need to separate. Because just like *Groundhog Day*, these issues will keep repeating until people have a good, hard look at themselves, their partner and what the real issues are. If nothing changes, then nothing changes.

On the other hand, everyone knows couples who divorce or separate, only to form another marriage or union where they've learned their lessons about what to do and what not to do, and the new partner benefits from this new level of emotional intelligence and knowledge. The old partner, who cried the tears, stuck it out and begged for change, has to watch as their ex goes on to be the partner they always dreamt of.

I wanted to address these negative patterns of dysfunction and help people create a new relationship. But rather than seeing clients create this new relationship with other people, I wanted them to do the work needed to recreate their current relationship.

Having survived failed relationships myself and making my share of mistakes, I know firsthand the emotional and financial trauma involved in a separation, and I wanted to create a dynamic, no-BS way of addressing relationship issues. I wanted to stop these negative loops that kept repeating from one relationship to the next, and I wanted couples to learn how to make the necessary changes to bring their relationship back to health. In other words, to resuscitate the relationship they're in right now rather than leaving and hoping for a better one.

I knew there had to be a more effective way of finding out if a relationship could, or should, be saved and discover if it's viable. A way to hit the reset button to change the interplay and dynamics and get down to the business of saving the relationship.

Wouldn't it be great for partners who have endured relationship hardship to be the ones to benefit from lessons learned? Oftentimes, they can. I've developed a deal-breaker model of couples counselling that aims to do just that. Fix behaviours and negative loops currently at play, so a new relationship can be created with the same partners. Over the many years I've been in private practice, it's become increasing apparent to me that couples need a relationship self-help guide that's solution focused, easy to understand, flushes out the commitment level on behalf of both parties, gets results and most importantly, is doable. It's all well and good to read about different theories and go through tick-and-flick questionnaires in an effort to assign a problem or a label to you or your partner's issues such as, "Oh he's a narcissist! He ticked eighteen out of twenty on the narcissist tick-and-flick quiz" or "Now I see she's just like her mother, because she's modelling her mother's crazy behaviour that she watched all through her childhood."

I feel these types of fix-it-yourself endeavours are rarely worthwhile or helpful, and my intention is to give a clear and easy-to-follow method of relationship repair I've used in private practice for years with great success. I decided to save couples from the pitfalls of going to not-for-profit organisations for relationship help. I can't tell you the number of times couples have come to see me after going to couples counselling with big organisations. As they explain their experience to me they often outline a familiar story that goes something like this:

"Well, we went to see our counsellor Carol, and after waiting six weeks for the appointment, we poured out all of our troubles, our deep, dark secrets and fears, picked open the deep wounds, cried a lot, and then went back a week later for our follow-up appointment. We were then led into a room with another counsellor, Bill, who calmly says, "Carol doesn't work here anymore. She's:

- *on holidays*

- *been transferred*

- *been promoted*

- *on maternity leave*

So, let's start from the beginning. What were your problems again?"

It doesn't take a rocket scientist to work out that this counselling relationship is going nowhere and not rendering any real, tangible help. More likely it will cause harm, because the couple involved often lose faith in the counselling process altogether. It's unfortunate that couples who seek counselling are forced into the cheaper organisational model due to financial hardship. They don't realise there's bona fide help to be had, often in only a few sessions, that would in fact be financially viable.

Other times only one partner can attend relationship counselling, and although it's still worthwhile for them to get help on their own, some people won't consider this option. Other barriers may be the elder system and religious constraints that prevent couples from seeking help outside of the elder or church structure.

Another constant I've seen is where one person wants to go to relationship counselling and the other refuses to go, because they don't want to hang out their dirty laundry to a stranger or feel counselling is a load of croc. As a consequence, the person who wants the counselling may come on their own and on behalf of their partner, to debrief and gain some strategies. However, this is not ideal, because counselling would then be focused on the individual, with a prioritised goal of ascertaining what would be the best outcome for them rather than for the union.

As I've said, there are many reasons why couples don't access adequate professional help when their relationship is in trouble. With these issues in mind, I have what I believe to be a workable relationship self-help guide. What you will get are real insights into what causes and maintains conflict. I don't participate in psychobabble and clichés. I will help point you in the right direction to change your behaviour, rethink your positions and heal your relationship. My message is of promise and hope that there really can be another way.

Chapter ♡ 1

THE DISPOSABLE SPOUSE

Drinks too much

Plays Golf every spare minute

Spends money we don't have

Won't try to get along with my family

Hates Intimacy

Too needy

Cheater

Chapter 1

♥

THE DISPOSABLE SPOUSE

- The Culture of Cut and Run

- People Are Not Penguins

- People Are Organisms

- There Are No Knights in Shining Armour

- Why People Don't Rescue Themselves

- The Case for Pre-cohabitation Conversations

Relationships can be difficult and highly disposable. People will go through many long-term relationships and/or marriages in their lifetime. It used to be a nightmare to get out of a marriage, and it was too hard to contemplate in some cases. The fears often were:

- Where will I go?

- How will I cope financially?

- Will I lose the kids, friends and support from family?

For some, this is still the case. But for the most part it's far easier to discard a relationship now than it was for previous generations. There are many more shelters, and government assistance is available to make leaving much easier to consider, plan for and take action towards.

THE CULTURE OF CUT AND RUN

Take The Family Law Act of 1975. It changed legalities regarding divorce law (dissolution of marriage) in this country in a revolutionary way. It replaced the fault grounds with irretrievable breakdown, which is established by a separation and the couple living apart for a period of just one year. And for a *decree nisi* divorce, which is a document that states the court doesn't see any reason why you can't divorce, the law reduced the time it takes effect from three months to just one. Sir Paul Coleridge, a well-respected judge who handled the divorce of Sir Paul and Heather McCartney said, "A cultural revolution has made it possible to end a marriage quickly with a basic form-filling exercise. Obtaining a divorce is now easier than getting a driving licence." (*Daily Mail Australia* January 23, 2016)

Internet dating has made it so much easier to find a replacement partner or sex and adventure with no commitment. This is in stark contrast to the past where trawling bars, clubbing, barbecues and friend hook-ups were the only way to meet someone new and hopefully better. There's often a recycling of partners others have left behind. These people go into a recycled relationship with the hope they will be a good fit, or as many and ex-wife has lamented, that they have benefited from realising they had issues to work on and developed more emotional intelligence by learning from their previous relationship mistakes. So, are we a culture of cut and run? Do couples find it easier to pack up and leave rather than to try to work things out? I think so.

PEOPLE ARE NOT PENGUINS

There's one fundamental idea I think everyone should realise. Humans are animals, and just like all animals, each is different with different behaviours. There are some animals that mate for life like penguins, black swans, vultures, turtle doves and French angel fish, to name a few. Humans are not animals that mate for life, and staying together is a mindful, ongoing commitment. If relationships are to survive, they must be fed and watered and tended to with love, respect, equity and consideration. Make no mistake. The playing field has changed.

It's much harder for relationships to survive in today's climate where access to others is so easy. The internet has bought social media into the home and given ready access to not only other people, but also easily accessible pornography and alternative-reality relationships and dating sites. One dating site slogan I've learned about is, *Life's short. Have an Affair* and promises confidentiality, so there are many options readily available. A person can easily be sexting or texting another love interest and carrying on affairs whilst at home with their spouse. Separation and divorce today are far more real threats than at any other time. Couples have to work at their relationship every day.

Recent research has uncovered that your personality continues to change through adulthood, so it's no big leap to understand that just as you're changing, so is your partner, and you may discover that even though you were a compatible match for each other some years ago, this may not continue to be the case now or in the future.

PEOPLE ARE ORGANISMS

All living things are organisms, including people. Just as plants grow towards that which nurtures them, like the sun, rain and nutrients, people will grow towards that which gives them the feeling of being worthwhile, attractive, engaging, funny and intelligent. This means a person may not be looking to have an affair or a one-night stand, but they've been so starved of affection and validation that the minute someone thinks they're engaging and attractive, they may feel drawn to that person. Not only is it validating, but it's exciting and emotionally nourishing. Feelings long forgotten are stirred, and there's an awakening of spirit. Often there's no intent, but gradually a person who's been bored or felt unloved and unattractive will start to love this feeling and crave more of it. They may change their appearance, buy new clothes, lose weight, go to the gym and start taking pride in themselves, all the while having thoughts of the new interest overtaking all others. Part of what I do in my private practice is to work with couples to mend relationships, change behaviours and to even make the decision as to whether or not the relationship should be saved.

Through my years of working with couples, one thing has become crystal clear. An affair is rarely the sole cause of a marriage breakdown but rather a symptom of an already sick relationship. Now, there are always going to be both men and women who will engage in sexual activity outside of the marriage at every opportunity and won't let a wedding band stand in the way of a good time. However, in most cases if there's been an affair it's because the person who's stepped outside of the relationship has been exposed to a kind of self-esteem building validation they're not getting at home.

Sometimes people go unconscious and don't even notice they, or their partner, are becoming unhappy and just move through life staying together yet drifting apart. In some cases, it's only when a third party notices them and provides this much-needed attention that they start to realise they're unhappy and want out. Someone thinks they're witty and attractive and goes out of their way to chat to them. All of a sudden there's a reason to spend time on clothes, hair and conversation, because someone is noticing and wants to engage with them.

After many years of feeling anything but attractive, they will gravitate towards the attention and validation of a new person who awakens feelings of being attractive and worthwhile. Just like the plant, they grow towards that which is nourishing them, the new interest, and away from the partner who keeps them in the shade. If a person is getting no affection, no intimacy and no words of encouragement from their partner, they may have trouble turning away from someone who's offering it.

Most people don't have the presence of mind to say to themselves, *Hang on. I'm feeling attracted to this person outside of my marriage, and I need to evaluate why* or *I don't feel like my partner loves or appreciates me. Maybe we should get couples counselling.* It's far more likely they'll start off with no intention of doing anything wrong, but they do enjoy the fantasy of imagining what a relationship with this new person would be like. They think the flirting is harmless, and they would never do anything about it. However time passes and the fantasising gets stronger, and pretty soon they can think of nothing else but the new love interest, and an affair ensues.

Sadly, most couples wait until their relationship is in real trouble before getting professional help. Often they'll argue on and off for years, take each other for granted, and repeat the same old behavioural loops that have kept them in a kind of toxic dance for years. Sometimes people will only seek to work on issues when the relationship is wheels off in a ditch, and it's too late to rebuild after all of the hurt and negative events. There are circumstances where one person will try to work on the relationship for years whilst getting no improvement from their partner. Then one day they up and walk out, and their partner will claim they didn't know the situation was that bad. They were blindsided and had no clue their partner was considering leaving.

The problem here is that oftentimes a person will do their grieving whilst they're still in the relationship. They'll read books, try strategies and give it their all. Then when they're done, they're DONE! However, the other person is only just starting to move though the shock and grief of the relationship breakdown and can't understand how their partner can be so matter of fact, cold and ready to move on.

The message here is that humans are organisms and will eventually gravitate towards what they need. Don't wait until it's too late to start giving your partner the validations and conditions they need to thrive in the relationship.

THERE ARE NO KNIGHTS IN SHINING ARMOUR. YOU'LL HAVE TO SAVE YOURSELF.

From an early age you're constantly exposed to the myth of the perfect mate. Think about childhood fairy tales such as *Cinderella*, *Sleeping Beauty*, and *Beauty and the Beast*. Look at movies like *The Notebook*, *Must Love Dogs*, and *Serendipity* to name just a few. You're exposed to the idea that somewhere *out there* is the perfect soul mate. Someone who will rescue you from loneliness, isolation and sadness. Who will always get it right, never hurt your feelings and have your back.

Although men are often looking to replace their mothers or may want a Stepford Wife, females are particularly prone to fall for this myth and think, *One day my prince will come. My knight in shining armour will show up, and I will be happy. Once I find my soul mate, I can really start living.* These beliefs often cloud the reality of being in a real relationship, where hard work and constant consideration of your partner are the real indicators of a successful relationship. If you're constantly looking for Mr. or Ms. Perfect, Mr. or Ms. Right will walk right past you and out of your life, because they weren't even in your field of vision.

There are no perfect partners, because there are no perfect people. Even if there were a perfect person who wanted to spend their life with you, chances are there would be an expectation for you to be perfect as well. Look, people make mistakes, and they'll let you down. Your goal should be to find someone who's of a good and loving character, will treat you with supportive love and respect, learn from their mistakes and always have the intention of prioritising mutual happiness and support.

This is not as hard to achieve as you might think. If you learn the golden rule, *We teach people how to treat us,* if you're not being respected and treated well, you'll just remove yourself from that person or remove them from you. I believe that if everyone demanded nothing but respect and honesty, they would soon be surrounded by respectful and honest people.

Relationships shouldn't be a tough row to hoe. They should feel manageable and also challenging, but not difficult. There's a big difference between work and struggle. Work is putting effort into something worthwhile that's beneficial to you and others. Struggle is fighting, enduring, and wrestling and has no place in a healthy relationship. If you have to struggle to keep a relationship, stop struggling and let it go. It's not for you, because good relationships don't feel like you're fighting to keep them. Instead, they should feel like you're working at keeping them healthy and rewarding. Once you lay this groundwork, you will have developed a code of ethics both of you will trust.

WHY PEOPLE DON'T RESCUE THEMSELVES

No one goes into a marriage believing it will fail. Often people will stay in a marriage, because they don't want to be the person who's had a second or third marriage. They don't want to tell their family they couldn't make it work or they mistakenly stay in a loveless union thinking they're taking the high road by honouring the *til death do us part* vow, or they remain tied by some other invisible ropes such as religious expectation.

There's often a belief that staying together is best for the kids. Children are far better at picking up hostility than most people imagine, even in their early years. They need a loving and supportive environment to optimally develop. Many will stay for financial reasons or to maintain the lifestyle and trappings that come with the marriage. Sometimes a title can be a huge draw card for people to stay in unhealthy unions. They don't want to lose the prestige of being married to a doctor, a professor or a celebrity, because they feel this link to the upper echelons gives them credibility.

Sometimes the reverse is true. A professional may be worth an absolute mint but won't go down the path of separation, because their partner never worked, and they'll be damned if they're going to pay spousal support and hand over half, or more, of their assets. So they stay in a miserable marriage with a partner they don't even like, let alone love.

Another constant is that some people can't bear the thought of losing extended family and friends, and they stay for social and support reasons, because leaving is scary. After all, there was no plan to start again, and maybe there's no confidence they can make it on their own. This is especially true of women who've gone straight from their parents' house into marriage. The plan was to have kids and make a good home. There's no extended education or career to fall back on, so they stay. Lots of clients confide to me they stay because they're not as young and attractive as they once were. They've gained weight, gotten softer and have lines and talk of other negative self-perceptions. Their belief is, "Who would want me now?" There's a great fear of loneliness and isolation that keeps people stuck. The children may have moved away, there's no more mothering to do, friends are linked to their partners and they may have no living or nearby family of origin to connect with.

A vital piece of information people who choose to endure a miserable marriage need to know is that they have no idea how damaging this can be to their health and happiness. Sociologists report that a stressful and upsetting marriage can be aligned with a greater occurrence of cardiovascular disease in both sexes, particularly those of advanced years. It's been reported this greater occurrence is especially true for females. The reasoning is that although most women are great communicators and often debrief with friends, they also tend to push down feelings and bottle them up, which leads to more stress and in turn may produce more cardiovascular issues.

Given the right information to make an educated choice, I believe far more people would end unsatisfying marriages/relationships to pursue more rewarding and loving partnerships, and in so doing, obtain a better life. If you're in a struggling, toxic or unhappy relationship, you should see if the relationship can be turned around to be supportive and loving, but if it can't you should rescue yourself by ending the union.

Low Self-Esteem and Staying in a Dysfunctional Relationship

When someone thinks about who they *should* or *ought* be, it can rob them of the confidence to leave a toxic relationship. They have a negative self image, are constantly on a diet, spend thousands of dollars a year on clothes or get-fit-quick gimmicks and always try to change into what they feel is a more acceptable person. Many women won't wear a swimsuit, let their partner see them naked and are always putting themselves down. The relationship suffers in the long term as they decide to settle for the partner they have right now, no matter how difficult or hurtful they can be, rather than to put themselves *out there* on the dating scene again.

Consider this: self-value is not a metric equation.

To compare one thing with another, a metric system must be used to quantify difference. However, no good or bad trait can be accurately measured. How could loyalty, a kind heart, good intent or an innate talent possibly be measured? Making comparisons is a mug's game! People who engage in this futile behaviour often face the problem of where to stop the comparison. There's no end to the number of comparisons you can make: beauty, social status, wealth, health, children, career achievements, skill, intelligence, and athleticism, just to name a few.

Don't exhaust yourself with this futile exercise. I encourage my clients who are suffering low self-esteem and see themselves as low achievers to use the concept of *The Gap* and not to always reach for ideals. I first heard about this way of explaining how to measure self-success years ago when I listened to Bill Harris in one of his recorded seminars. I've since used it as a self-esteem-building strategy with great success. In using counselling strategies called *Re-Storying* and *Re-framing*, which I'll explain later, the idea of The Gap aligns with these ideas.

The Gap involves looking back to see how far you've come, or the gap between then and now, rather than looking ahead to see if you're there yet. By *there*, I'm referring to the idealistic version of the world, which like the horizon, seems to advance in direct relation to your efforts to reach for it. If you use The Gap concept, you will see more clearly the positives you've achieved in your life rather than be totally focused on what you've yet to achieve.

For instance, you may have had a child, bought a house, advanced in your job, made new contacts and learned more about yourself. Are you the healthiest you've ever been? If so, what have you done differently, and what could you do to increase your health even more? Or if it's worse, what changed? There's nothing wrong with self-growth and wanting to better yourself, but it must be done for you and not to compete with the often unrealistic standards dictated by others, such as Hollywood and the media.

In life, you need to back yourself. Start being your own best friend, and get on your own side. You should spend time in reflection of your behaviours to better yourself and stop those that no longer serve you. Become conscious, but never beat yourself up. If you struggle with self-esteem issues that interfere with your relationships, realise that the struggle may have nothing to do with your self-value or appearance and everything to do with behaviours driven by low self-esteem.

I'll explore archetypes more later, but for now I'll just talk about the archetype of the victim. There are some people who get stuck in relationship mistreatment and fail to rescue themselves, because they can't get their head around the unfairness of it all. They play the role of the hapless victim who's undeservedly mistreated and wallow in a *That shouldn't happen* victim mentality. This way of dealing with issues is to not deal with them at all but rather be righteous about what trespasses have come their way. They may tell anyone and everyone about how they've been cheated, swindled, and abandoned, and how crushed they are over being a victim. Often these people stay inert and won't fight for their rights or rescue themselves.

What's interesting about those who play the victim is that they'll only complain about that which they have a choice about and not what's fixed and out of their control. For instance, you don't hear anyone complaining about gravity or where the sun rises and sets. They don't go around saying, "Oh, this gravity is really upsetting me. I throw things up, and they come straight back down." Most adults have options regarding their issues, but they fail to exercise a healthy choice.

The truth is that if you want to change your life, you have to simply accept that bad things happen to good people. No, it isn't fair, but being inactive and lying on the floor whinging your life away is not the answer. Sometimes in life you have to get up on your hind legs and fight for your rights in a *take no prisoners* kind of way, and sometimes you have to do this when you're in a dysfunctional and abusive relationship.

Dr Phil McGraw talks about this issue in his book, *Life Strategies*, where he recounts a story of when he was working as a trial strategist with Oprah and her trial lawyer Charles (Chip) Babcock. Oprah was in the fight of her life to defend herself against a beef industry lawsuit in Amarillo, Texas. Oprah is nobody's victim, but this story goes to show how even the most evolved of us can get pulled into the trap of *This shouldn't be happening* thinking.

Dr Phil described how Oprah continued to struggle with the unfairness and the *why* of it all. She'd done nothing wrong, and the ranchers were gunning for her with civil charges of fraud and negligence, among others. Dr Phil helped Oprah turn this thinking around so that instead of getting caught up in the unfairness, she started to fight for her rights, her reputation and the truth.

So, if you're with someone who treats you unfairly, examine why you stay. Are you attached to playing the role of the victim, or are you just numb and unconscious about how you can, and should, rescue yourself?

The good news is that you can always change behaviours that are not in your best interest. Be balanced in your thinking and spend time appreciating who you are and all of your positive attributes, rather than what you think is wrong with you. If you experience low self-esteem, personal counselling can give you more of the tools and strategies to build your self-worth and move forward in life. Nothing is more attractive than confidence. As the old saying goes, *You have to be yourself, because everyone else is taken.*

A CASE FOR PRE-COHABITATION DISCUSSIONS

When I do pre-marriage/cohabitation counselling, I explore with both parties what potential problems might look like. Counselling is not just for when things go pear shaped. It's worthwhile to do as soon as a relationship gets serious. Once a couple start to make plans to share a life, they should consider the future and how best to ensure they're on the same page.

I recommend premarital or pre-cohabitation counselling where you both talk about expectations on a variety of matters, including money, rules for managing each other's family, vacations and visions for the future to name just a few. Here you can have the hard conversations about fidelity, what each of you considers cheating and those practices you'll put in place to protect the relationship.

There's a strong argument for pre-marriage/cohabitation counselling, and I don't mean by elders or your place of worship where the pastor, rabbi, priest, padre, or the like may not have recognised and up-to-date qualifications. To be comprehensive and non-biased, these discussions and negotiations need to be a collaborative exercise carried out by a fully qualified counsellor who can guide you through all of the issues that are likely to arise in a lifelong union. After all, a lifetime union is the objective of getting married or setting up a life together in the first place, isn't it?

If I had the power, I would make three pre-marital counselling sessions with a fully qualified therapist mandatory as part of the process of registering for marriage, and six counselling sessions before being granted a divorce. By the simple act of investing in the premarital counselling process, I believe the divorce rate would at least halve in number, because couples would get down to the business of looking at compatibility, and then either adjust expectations and make a plan or rethink the idea of getting married in the first place.

Those in the process of getting a divorce may have cause to rethink and instead commit to finding out if the union can be saved if they go to counselling, get clarity and do the work. Many couples will start out believing love will conquer all, and then when everything goes wrong, make excuse after excuse for behaviours that are not conducive to a successful outcome. I've been counselling couples for many years, and I can say the dynamic set up early in the relationship is the one that tends to stay forever, or until the couple seek professional intervention.

For instance, if one partner keeps quiet about topics that matter, makes excuses for the other partner such as, "He/she's just tired and didn't mean what they said or did" and hopes they'll grow out of bad behaviours or that the situation will simply right itself, that's setting the status quo for the relationship going forward. Both parties need to be crystal clear about what's deemed fair and equitable, and this is where pre-marriage/cohabitation counselling is a real benefit for those choosing a life together.

Lots of couples decide to come together, buoyed by dreams and expectations that are never discussed or really communicated to each other. Romance and the heady early days of being in love can overshadow the hard reality of everyday life that's so often out of the field of vision. At this stage, no one wants to have the hard conversations about the many issues that can, and do, impact a marriage or lifelong union. There needs to be a commitment on behalf of both parties to protect, nurture and grow the relationship, and to do this, hard conversations are needed.

If you look at some of the issues I make sure to cover in pre-marital/ cohabitation sessions, you can easily see how going through this process puts couples in the most favourable position for success. Examples of lifelong goals and shared expectations pre-marriage include:

- mutual expectations around gender roles, such as domestic duties and home maintenance

- number of children

- possible pregnancy issues or if there's a child with special needs

- beliefs around terminating a pregnancy

- infertility

Would each partner be open to fertility treatment such as IVF, along with the associated financial commitment?

- parenting and discipline views

For established unions this includes boundaries and expectations around stepchild/children, both youngsters and adults.

- education choices: private vs. public

- financial management, including budgeting and boundaries around lending to family and friends

- parents and parent in-law management

- lending money

Yes or no? And if so, how much?

- gifts limits, donations and charity work

- intimacy and communication

- resolving heated arguments

- spiritual life.

- the parameters of cheating

Is it only sexual betrayal, or is it also friendships with the opposite sex, confiding in others, or sharing personal information?

- house purchase, superannuation and retirement plans

Does one of you think it would be a good idea to tour around the country in retirement, while the other sees this as a slow roast in hell?

> **"Relationships are negotiated, and if you deal with ultimatums and authority all the time, then you're not going to get anywhere."**
>
> DR PHIL

One of the great advantages of premarital counselling is that hard conversations about hard topics can be addressed and planned for in a supportive environment before the situation becomes heated and emotionally loaded. Cool heads that are still in the honeymoon phase can make solid plans. In therapy you can identify the land mines of a relationship before someone stands on one of them and causes a blowout in the relationship. Even when couples have done the work, been to premarital counselling and are full of good intent, there are still many traps and potholes a couple can run into. However, having a plan of action should always make the resolution easier.

Some people are naïve enough to see all of the flaws but just hope the situation will get better, or they can change their partner. They may blindly believe that love will conquer all, and their love will make things right. Sadly, this is almost always not the case.

Next I'll explore why relationships get into trouble and why so often nothing is done about it.

Chapter ♡ 2

WHY IT ALL GOES WRONG AND DOESN'T GET BETTER

Chapter 2

♥

WHY IT ALL GOES WRONG AND DOESN'T GET BETTER

- Thinking the Situation Will Get Better in Time

- Playing the Passive-Aggressive Game

- Building Resentments

- The Artful Dodger

- The Poached Frog Syndrome

- Developing Patterns of Dysfunctional Communication

- Failure to Plan for Inevitable Changes

- Planning for Retirement

The descent into relationship failure can be slow and often doesn't attract much attention until it's well on the way to being too late. Days, months and years go by, each folding into the next, and life becomes routine and predictable, with couples largely zoning out. Then one day they realise they're unhappy, marriage is not as they envisioned when they got together and they often have no idea how they got to this uncomfortable and unhappy place.

To best plan for a happy life with your partner, you need to know where the land mines are, so let's explore what some of these are before you step on them.

THINKING THE SITUATION WILL GET BETTER IN TIME

Thinking situations will get better in time if you just leave them alone or telling yourself to just give it time while taking no action, can lead to a belief that the universe is unfolding as it should and everything will work out for the higher good. Investing in this kind of belief can have the effect of taking your control of the situation away and have you and your partner abdicating any responsibility for how your lives turn out.

This kind of thinking encourages complacency and stops you from being proactive in designing your life and levels of happiness and satisfaction. Every bit of self-improvement study I've engaged in, experiences I've had and evidence I've collected, demonstrates to me that the universe is largely neutral, and life rewards action.

You have to actively manage your life, make decisions, try different strategies and set collaborative goals with your partner to make a result happen and create the future you want. Life will always throw you challenges, but if you're proactive and engage in solution-focused thinking, you will naturally undertake personal growth and become better and better at negotiating and overcoming these challenges.

If you settle for a life that's not so great, you will usually get a life that's not so great. You have to believe there can be a brighter future and take the necessary steps to find your way there. If nothing changes, then nothing changes. If you don't get proactive, grow, and learn from your past to better manage your future, than you will continue to hope for the best rather than going about the business of creating it.

Problems rarely, if ever, get better by throwing time at them. You may believe that if you just wait it out, the situation will magically get better. Don't listen to well-meaning people who say "Give it time" and "Don't worry, it'll all work out in the end." Life needs to be managed, and you need to take responsibility for your actions, or lack of action. You won't hear a pilot with an engine cutting out say, "I'm sure it'll all work out in the end." NO. He takes action to do all he can to save the situation, and so should you. It's always better to be proactive than reactive but especially important in managing your relationships.

PLAYING THE PASSIVE-AGGRESSIVE GAME

Often communication gets so poor, couples start to play the passive-aggressive game. Passive-aggressive behaviours typically develop in early childhood and can become a huge issue in relationships. A passive-aggressive way of behaving can be largely unconscious, and although a person may basically be nice and have integrity and lots of friends, they hurt others or themselves with little or no knowledge about what they're actually doing. This kind of behaviour can be a way of dealing with anger and getting retribution against those who've wronged them without having to face a confrontation. Passive-aggressive people may have absolutely no idea this is how they've learned to process anger.

- He will say, *"What's wrong, honey?"* and she will say, *"Nothing"* while all the while seething, because he forgot her birthday.

- He will deliberately pretend he forgot to take out the bins in the morning, knowing his wife will do it before she goes to work. She will suspect he does it deliberately but never say anything.

- She promises she will make plans for them both on the weekend but then decides to go out with the girls. She may even justify this by saying to herself, *If he can't even remember my birthday, then I can't be too important to him, so I'll just go out with my friends who do give a damn.*

Passive-aggressive behaviour is about the furthest thing there is from teamwork and a cohesive friendship, and there's no healthy place for it in a relationship. Some behaviours that are passive-aggressive in nature are:

- giving someone the silent treatment

- sulking

- deflecting blame

- being clingy and over-dependant

- punishing in subtle ways without confronting the issue

- deliberately making mistakes

- deliberately arriving late to keep people waiting

- resenting any demands and believing any expectations are unfair

- making double-meaning jokes as a way of venting at someone

- dressing criticism as a compliment

- always needing to have the last word

- moaning of feeling unappreciated or put upon

It's more than worthwhile to take some time to consider these traits to see if you can recognise any of them in the way you or your partner operate. If you both decide to be transparent and honest about what you're feeling, thinking and doing, the relationship would become all it could be, and if it's not working out, it would be discovered sooner rather than later. This allows you to take steps to either work on the relationship or call an end to it. Without honesty and transparency in the union, there's nothing to work with.

Now, when I talk about honesty and transparency, I don't mean you have to disclose every waking thought, conversation or details of your day, but *you should* disclose thoughts and feelings that relate to the relationship. You're in it together, and you each have the right to know about anything that's affecting the health of the relationship.

BUILDING RESENTMENTS

Resentments get established early in a relationship and continue to grow over time. Here are some reasons this might happen:

- She wants children but he didn't, so she gave up the idea of motherhood for the relationship.

- He wanted to take his career overseas, but she wouldn't move away from her mother.

- She wanted to study, but he thought it a waste of time and wanted her to focus on the home and caring for the children.

- He wanted to travel and live a little before getting a mortgage and having children, and she wanted to buy some land and start looking at display homes and travel when the kids leave home.

I often see clients who give up one dream, only to learn that it will be the first of many. All relationships must have compromise, but the compromise should be on both sides, fair and well-considered. Couples will agree to all kinds of adaptations in their life plan whilst in the glow of a new romance, but time kills the honeymoon phase, reality sets in and the business of everyday life may see couples reviewing what they gave up and wondering if it was all worth it.

THE ARTFUL DODGER

If you would rather stay away than go home, something is terribly wrong. If you go to work early, dawdle, go to pubs, sporting clubs, coffee houses or shops to delay getting home, your relationship is in big trouble. Likewise, if you're always getting home late, are busy on the weekend and over-committed elsewhere with anyone and everyone but your partner, there's something you need to confront. You need to be honest with yourself and your partner as to why you're avoiding time together. Have feelings changed? You need to talk about the issues and behaviour/s driving a wedge between you and your partner. In short, there's a need to identify the reason/s for the growing distance between you and start working on the problem instead of letting the problem work you.

As discussed earlier, these kinds of avoidance issues rarely, if ever, get better on their own. If sexual frequency has changed, and there are no efforts to make contact with even small affections such as hugs and cuddling, there's a problem. When avoidance occurs in a relationship, there's always a reason. Avoidance could signal an affair with sexual needs being met elsewhere, or it could signal a medical issue such as depression or erectile dysfunction, where embarrassment may cause avoidance of intimate situations. In the case of a personality change, it could be due to the side-effects of a new medication. Weight loss drugs may cause grumpiness, a short temper, or crying and a lack of interest in sex. If a personality change is fairly recent, there needs to be some investigation around why there's been a change rather than just assuming it's not important. The point is that avoidance always means something, and one of you has to be brave enough to force the issue.

THE POACHED FROG SYNDROME

Some people will stay in a toxic relationship for literally years and years, because the gradual passing of time prevents them from realising the truth about the extent of unhappiness they've been enduring. Years of increasing mistreatment, put downs, dismissive treatment, enforced controlling demands, and possibly abuse may have started out as only an occasional event, but after a while the mistreatment gradually became the relationship norm.

I see these types of issues regularly in the counselling room, and I refer to it as *The Poached Frog Syndrome*. The explanation of this syndrome goes like this: if you catch a frog and throw him into a pot of boiling water, he will most certainly jump out. However, if you put the frog in a pot of tepid water and then slowly, over time, turn up the heat, the frog may find the warm water comforting and soothing at first, and it may adjust itself constantly in line with the variations of the extreme conditions. In this way he increases his tolerance of discomfort and learns to live with it. However, one day that frog will either die from being poached, or he will jump out to save his life.

People who are in the process of being poached may try to make excuses for the negative behaviours of a partner. They may tell themselves, *It's the alcohol talking, and she didn't mean it* or *He doesn't want me to go out without him, because he worries about me* or *He's right, I don't really need new clothes. It's just a waste of good money.* These people make an art form out of rationalising every hurt away, so they can live with it. The truth is that they're not rationalising but rather telling themselves "rational lies."

DEVELOPING PATTERNS OF DYSFUNCTIONAL COMMUNICATION

Communication is made up of two elements: the *sender* and the *receiver*. For communication to be successful, the receiver must receive the message as the sender intended.

It's common to say something innocent but for your partner to interpret the statement as negative, even where there's no such negative intent. A glance, a turn of a head or a gesture can mean absolutely nothing relevant to the topic at hand or be in any way aimed at the receiver, but oftentimes these innocent asides are misread as sarcasm, dismissal or contempt.

Some of my clients are especially talented at creating a whole narrative in their head about what *never* happened. At these times I'm always reminded of a cartoon picture I saw in the seventies. In this illustration a couple is lying in bed, and they both have think bubbles above their heads. The woman's think bubble reads, *He's so quiet. He hasn't spoken to me for ages. I bet he's upset I bought that new dress. He's probably thinking I'm spending his money. Well screw him! This is my money, too, and I'll spend whatever I damn well like. Dad was right. He's selfish to the core!*

Inside his bubble was a tune he was trying to remember:

♪♫♪♫ *"Flintstones.....Meet the Flintstones....."* ♪♫♪♫

When these types of miscommunications happen constantly, hate grows for the person exhibiting imagined behaviour, instead of what's really going on. In these cases, simple communication skills such as *paraphrasing* and *checking for understanding* can turn the whole miscommunication problem around in a short time.

For instance, if she sees a roll of the eyes or what she perceives as a dismissive gesture, she can check for understanding by saying something like, "When you roll your eyes like that, it makes me think you're fed up with me. Is that what you're feeling?" He then has the opportunity to either say, "Yes, I'm fed up with you. That's exactly what I'm feeling" or "No, honey. I'm fed up with the situation, not you."

Another example of asking for clarification is the use of paraphrasing. He says, "I'm over the whole thing," and she says "So, you're saying you're over the marriage, is that right?" He can then either clarify if he was talking about the fighting, the situation, or that he was indeed talking about the marriage. These two communication strategies alone are effective in clearing up intentions, bad feelings and other miscommunication within the union.

You should also be on the lookout for *futurerising* and *catastrophising* behaviours. This is the tendency to talk using catastrophic and emotionally loaded language by declaring, "If things don't change soon, I'm going to die" or "We're all doomed to Hell" and "I just can't bear one more minute of this!" A person who uses this kind of language affects everyone around them in a negative way and can alter the mood of others from happy or neutral to dreadful.

Communication is not always verbal, and in fact most is nonverbal. It's interesting to note that Dr. Albert Mehrabian, the author of *Silent Messages,* undertook multiple studies on nonverbal communication. His findings reflected that only seven percent of any given message is conveyed through words, thirty-eight percent is conveyed through particular vocal elements, and fifty-five percent is through nonverbal elements that include facial expressions, physical gestures, and posture. So if you take away the seven percent for actual words spoken, this leaves a ninety-three percent statistic of all communication being nonverbal. Ninety-three percent!

With this astounding figure, you can see why it's so important to work on communication skills and where there's doubt, check for understanding. As you look at the statistics regarding nonverbal communication, it's no wonder that texts and emails are fertile ground for misunderstandings between couples, because they only contain words, and words can be interpreted in many ways.

Some people say capitals are for emphasis, and others say it's to indicate yelling. Women will often end an email where they're trying to explain how they feel with dozens of exclamation marks. Men may stare at this like a cat watching clothes go around in the dryer, wondering what in the world she's on about. The meaning isn't clear, because the sender has failed to send the message in a way the receiver can decode. So with this in mind, don't carry on fighting via text messages, and don't try to put forward your case or explain how you feel in an email, because there's a high chance it won't achieve what you intended and could make the situation a whole lot worse.

My light bulb moment about misreading a partner came about around twenty years ago. I can still remember it as though it was last week. My son, who was about seven at the time, was standing in the doorway looking out at some kids playing in the outdoor area of a childcare centre I was working in at that time. I noticed he was displaying the same body gestures and facial grimace I'd seen many times in his father and always assumed was sarcastic or dismissive behaviour. This is how I learned this grimace, which he still has, is his concentrating facial expression and nothing else. I then realised I'd assigned a lot of nastiness to his father that wasn't deserved.

There's a great list of communication barriers devised by Thomas Gordon (Parent Effectiveness Training, 1970, pp. 4147, 108117, and 32127). Thomas wrote that one of the main reasons communication fails to be effective is due to people inserting barriers or blockers into their conversations without realising it. He calls his comprehensive list *The Dirty Dozen* and clearly outlines twelve of the most common communication barriers people use. This list has been utilised by many professionals, including counsellors, mediators, CEOs, childcare workers, and human resource officers to ensure best practices in communication. I always make sure my counselling students learn them well. I've reproduced them for you here:

1. Ordering, directing, commanding

Instructing the person as to what they have to do, using bully language such as, "You must," "You should" and "You will" in the form of an order. This is likely to create fear, and often retaliation.

2. Warning, threatening, promising

Threatening a person with a negative consequence or rewarding them with the promise of something positive. "If you don't like it ..." or "You'd better do what I ask or else..." This can induce fear and submissiveness, as well as anger, resentment and retaliation.

3. Moralising, preaching, shoulds and oughts

This means preaching to a person using sanctimonious speech and moralising. "You should...," "You ought to ...," "You need to...," "You're obliged to do it." This often brings on feelings of guilt and untrustworthiness.

4. Sending solutions, advising or strongly suggesting

Advising a person as to how to go about solving an issue or constantly throwing out suggestions. Making statements like, "What I would do is...," "Why don't you try it this way..." and "I'm just going to put this out there…" can lead a person to feel they're not capable of solving their own issues and can prevent them from working through the problem and developing problem-solving skills. This can cause dependency or retaliation.

5. Teaching, lecturing, giving logical arguments

This barrier is where someone tries to use logic, data, opinion, facts and argumentative language to influence a person. "This is where you're going wrong...," "The facts tell us that..." and "Yes, but...." This kind of communication can be adversarial and provoke a defensive response with counter-arguments, which ends up with the receiver experiencing feelings of inadequacy. They may start to use disengaging or whiting-out noise to not listen to the sender, and then no effective listening or communication can take place.

6. Judging, criticising, disagreeing, blaming.

This kind of communication is where someone makes a negative judgment or evaluation of another. "You're not thinking clearly...," "You have baby brain" or "That's just the hormones talking." This type of exchange implies incompetence, idiocy and poor judgment and usually ends useful communication due to the receiving party being in fear, feeling judged or being told off. The argument can go in circles, and in the end the receiver will say something like, "Sure, you can talk! Look at the mess your life is in!"

7. Praising, agreeing

This means placating and assuring someone that what they're doing is just great. A person using praising and agreeing will always assess a situation as positive. An example would be, "Wow! You really are great at your job!" or "I agree. That person sounds like an idiot!" This kind of exchange sets high expectations and monitoring of a person hitting a high mark all of the time. It can be interpreted as patronising, controlling or manipulative to illicit a desired response from the receiver. In children it can be particularly stressful if they don't believe they can keep performing at such a high standard and have anxiety about letting people down.

8. Shaming, ridiculing, chastising

Here there's a tendency to make a person out to be an idiot by labelling them in a derogatory way using shaming and self-image-destroying phrases such as idiot, cry baby, wimp, and know-it-all. This kind of communication can make a person feel incompetent and severely affect their self-esteem and belief in themselves to cope. Above all, it destroys relationships.

9. Interpreting, analysing, diagnosing

Here there's a tendency to tell the receiver what his or her motives are, or to provide a reason why the person says something or behaves in a certain way. It communicates that the sender has the receiver's number and knows the motivation or causation for their position. The language of this kind of communication is diagnostic. For example, "You know what your problem is, don't you? It's that…," "It's your mother who made you like you are…" or "You don't really mean that, what you really mean is…" This type of communication can be frustrating and drives the receiver to seek distance from the sender, because they feel trapped, exposed, or that they're being called a liar.

10. Reassuring, sympathising, consoling, supporting

This kind of communication seeks to make the receiver feel better by talking them out of his or her negative feelings and stopping them from emoting while denying the strength of their feelings. "Don't worry about it," "Things always work out for the better," "Oh, come on, cheer up. Things will look better tomorrow" or "It's not that bad." This kind of communication causes a receiver to feel silly that they're feeling bad and misunderstood. It can also evoke negative feelings, such as hostility. The receiver may interpret this kind of exchange as someone telling them, "You don't have the right to be upset or sad."

11. Interrogating, probing, questioning

Here the sender tries to play detective by prying for more detailed information, such as reasons and motives, to help the receiver achieve a goal or solve a problem. They may ask, "Why did this happen?" "Who was there with you?" "So, what happened next, and what did you say?" or "How did you feel?" Since answering these questions often results in getting subsequent criticisms or solutions, the receiver often learns to reply in one-word, closed responses, or uses avoidance, exaggerations or lies. The effect of probing causes anxiety and fear or an inability to participate in the matter at hand.

12. Withdrawing, distracting, humouring, diverting

Here the sender tries to get the receiver to distance themselves from the problem by using distraction, joking or avoidance and only puts focus on what's working in the receiver's life. They may use phrases like, "Let's talk about good things" or "Why don't you take up a new hobby?" This type of communication implies that it's a good idea to not deal with your problems but rather sweep them under the carpet. This can trivialise a receiver's problems and does not build rapport.

FAILURE TO PLAN FOR INEVITABLE CHANGES

When two become more, change is inevitable. Many people underestimate the change a child will make to not only the marriage but their entire lives. All of a sudden you have a little person who's totally reliant on you for everything, and no matter how much a child is wanted and planned for, it can be a difficult adjustment for everyone.

Hormones and tiredness can make coping difficult, and many women feel that caring for their first child is the hardest task they've ever undertaken. Often men will feel neglected and be unreasonably upset, feeling like the baby takes all of the attention. The parent who stays at home to care for the baby, usually the mother, can become resentful because of the life their partner has outside of the home. They imagine the freedom, adult conversation and time away from a screaming baby, and indeed many young fathers have disclosed to me they do stay late at work, because they can't stand the baby noise.

When baby comes, there's little room for spontaneity. A simple trip to the shop becomes an excursion that requires planning and preparation, including stocked nappy bags, prams, umbrellas and all of the normal paraphernalia that comes with a new baby. Often young couples will isolate themselves and stay at home, because it's just easier than going out with the baby. There's often a tendency to lose friends, because they see the baby as a pain and a disruption, which further isolates the parents from adult stimulation and social activity.

Women may have to give up careers and aspirations, at least in the short term, and may also resent the body changes that occur after childbirth. Sexual activity can change due to tiredness, body image and loss of sex drive on both sides. Often men are resentful of the reduced sexual activity after childbirth, but they also discover they're no longer attracted to their wives, due to body changes such as stretch marks, lactating breasts and vaginal changes. Women sometimes react to these issues and develop low self-esteem. They begin to avoid intercourse and other activities they previously enjoyed but now make them feel exposed, such as showering together and getting undressed in front of their husbands.

Couples need to plan for inevitable changes when they decide to have children. Issues like domestic duties should be mapped out before baby comes and all practical matters planned for. There needs to be open and honest conversations about not only the upside of having children but also the real downside. This is where family planning counselling can really help couples prepare for parenthood. With realistic expectations, regular couple time and open communication, couples can make this transition time much easier. Taking a wait-and-see approach to marriage and parenting is a fool's game.

PLANNING FOR RETIREMENT

There's a false belief out there that only young couples ever need relationship help, but the truth is that more than half of the clients I see are baby boomers, and many of the issues are around managing retirement. All couples should spend time planning for retirement, because it can be one of the greatest challenges a marriage can face. There's a condition of sorts I call RSS, or Retired Spouse Syndrome, that can lead to depression and stress. After retirement, some people will start to interfere with issues previously managed by their partner.

This is especially true of spouses who held a supervisory position prior to retirement. They're used to dictating how things will go and may try to emulate the hierarchy in their own homes they once had at work. This never goes well and can be the cause of great disharmony in the marriage, just at a time when life is supposed to be getting easier.

Finances will often change and money, particularly how it's spent, can become a huge issue. The good news is that this often settles down once each person realises they must change the way they operate within the home, because there's no choice but to do so. Newly retired people need to adjust their expectations of having total say over everything at home, and their partners will have to come to terms with having to compromise. Conditions can't remain the way they were, because the situation has irreversibly changed.

Here are some ways for couples to ensure there's compromise while maintaining their own identity:

- Engage in independent activities enjoyed by each partner, such as hobbies, outings, family time and social engagements.

- Try to make some private real estate in the house. For instance, if she loves writing, have a room that's conducive to writing and privacy. If he loves playing an instrument, have a music room.

- Work out a reasonable budget based on the most likely reduced income and include funds for entertainment.

- Keep an attitude that's open to being fair and equitable, and be prepared to negotiate when there's opposition over big and small issues.

Chapter ♥ 3

THE CRITICAL STEPS ON THE PATH TO HEALING

Chapter 3

THE CRITICAL STEPS ON THE PATH TO HEALING

- The Mandatory Conditions for Success

- Becoming Conscious

- Become a Fortune Teller

- Forgive It or Forget It

- Stop Spreading the News

- Don't Believe the Evidence

- Your Home Should Be Your Sanctuary

THE MANDATORY CONDITIONS FOR SUCCESS

For couples to successfully create change in the relationship, there are mandatory conditions I believe are imperative.

First, both parties must still love each other. There are times when the situation has gotten so bad that people aren't sure if they're *in love*, but they must still love the person they're entering the process with. Apathy towards a partner or spouse just won't cut it.

I also often see one half of a couple who presents as aloof and disengaged and describe their feelings towards their partner, and life in general, as numb and empty. This can be emotional exhaustion, and there's a real need for this person's nervous system to have a time-out from the fighting and the toxic dance of fights and upsets. Sometimes a trial separation is in order.

Second, both parties must be prepared to do the work and change their behaviours. I strongly believe that on a fundamental level if someone truly loves their partner, they would be willing to change any behaviour that's causing them to be upset and is putting the relationship at risk. If there's no willingness to change these destructive behaviours, how can there be love? To be clear, I'm not talking about having people change *who they are* or to pretend to be something they're not. I'm saying that if there's a certain behaviour that's causing upset to their partner, they should be willing to change it.

It's rarely the case that one person is entirely responsible for the issues in a relationship, so a willingness from each partner to look at and change their behaviour is mandatory for success. That being said, one partner having alcoholism or other forms of addiction is the exception, but there will still be room for a behavioural adjustment on the partner's side to accommodate change.

There must be a commitment to hear what behaviours each partner considers deal breakers and a willingness to change them.

Remember, these behaviours wouldn't have the weight of being called a deal breaker on a contract if they didn't find the behaviour hurtful or detrimental. Deal breakers must be fair and equitable, and no party should be asked to behave in a way that's in conflict with their beliefs, morals or ethics. I would never consider a deal breaker that asked someone to be subservient, perform sexual acts they're not comfortable with, to be cut off from family or any other unethical request.

Third, is that both partners must make room for the belief the other can change. For instance, if there's an agreement where a behaviour has been earmarked for extinction by the husband, but he doesn't truly believe his wife can keep her commitment to change, the couple faces an uphill battle. It's hard to modify well-established behaviour, and it's even harder to make that change when someone is just waiting for the other to stuff up. When changing any behaviour, whether it's for relationship or personal reasons such as giving up eating junk food or to stop swearing or overspending, there will inevitably be slip ups on the way to success.

Imagine you're learning to touch type, and you're making progress. Now imagine demonstrating your touch typing with someone standing behind you, waiting and watching for you to make a mistake. Not really conducive to success, is it? Using this analogy, you can understand that if you feel like you're being constantly monitored for failure, and your partner is just waiting in the wings to pounce the second you backslide, you're less likely to succeed. This means it's important to understand that if you have a commitment to change, it may take a little time for the new behaviour to become established. If you're truly committed to saving a relationship, you will give your partner support while expecting some hiccups along the way. The goal is to establish consistent and noticeable change over the short term and not to expect immediate results.

Changing an ingrained behaviour takes time and commitment. Maxwell Maltz, in my view, may have led people astray when he published a statement in his 1960 book, *Psycho-Cybernetics*. In this book, Maltz stated that it takes a minimum of twenty-one days to form a habit. Over time, I believe people just forgot the "minimum" part of that statement, and so it became a misquote, repeated over and over again, leading many to believe that twenty-one days was the magic number. This is a falsity for most of us.

Maltz's book became a bestseller and went on to heavily influence the way behaviour formation and behaviour extinction was viewed. Over the past decades, this twenty-one day statement has been repeated time and time again by many professionals working in the self-help field. It was quoted so often, many people assumed it was a statistical fact.

So, what's the truth? Phillippa Lally is a health psychology researcher at University College London. In a study published in the *European Journal of Social Psychology*, Lally looked at the habits of ninety-six subjects across a three-month period. Her findings concluded that the real timeline to form a habit is sixty-six days. So, couples need to allow time for their partner to make a new behaviour instinctual.

Therapists have long understood that to successfully change an unwanted behaviour you need to replace it with a positive one.

There are three components to a habit or behaviour. First, there's a trigger for a well-worn behaviour. For instance, a husband might hear the ping of a Facebook update on his wife's phone just as they're sitting down to dinner. This causes him to tense his shoulders and his jaw to clench, because he's asked her a million times to *put the darn thing away.*

The belief feeds a behavioural loop or routine. What does he believe about the trigger? It could be that his wife doesn't prioritise time with him over social media, or that she doesn't enjoy his company, or a million other interpretations. In this case he might roll his eyes and start banging and clanging the dishes and cutlery. Then comes the reward, such as letting out frustrations, yelling and getting her to say she's sorry. The consequence is yet another argument and ruined dinner.

Somewhere in the mind, this pattern of behaviour is remembered, and the cycle becomes a constant feature of the relationship. In a therapeutic setting with a counsellor like myself, we would use Cognitive Behavioural Therapy to help a client recognise the triggers, the belief about the trigger and then revise the outcome by changing the belief. Couples can work through this A, B, C model of Cognitive Behavioural Therapy on their own, and there are literally hundreds of worksheets available online if you would like to use one yourself.

BECOMING CONSCIOUS

> "I know of no more encouraging fact
> than the unquestionable ability of
> man to elevate his life by conscious
> endeavor"

HENRY DAVID THOREAU

If you intentionally practice consciousness as you go through life, you'll have a choice about how events, people and emotions impact you. If you just go through life on autopilot, you will never be able to see which behaviours are serving you and which are bringing about the negative results. You go through life being largely unconscious of your actions and can do many unhelpful and unhealthy activities as you move through your days in this state. You can mindlessly eat rubbish, smoke cigarettes, use recreational drugs and fail to exercise, while being unaware of objects, people, and events right in front of you. For instance, as you mindlessly watch TV, stare at Facebook or get absorbed in a love affair or work, your child slips into depression.

Likewise, you can be living a good life, going to work, cooking dinner and socialising with friends and never notice your partner is slipping away into the arms of someone else. You need to mindfully practice being conscious, so you don't allow negative situations to happen, and this includes negating your responsibilities as a spouse, partner or parent while zoning out.

How many times have you heard people declare, "I had no idea he/ she was having an affair. I was the last to know." However, if they look back honestly they would have to admit to all kinds of signs, such as smelling a foreign shampoo or after supposedly working late, their partner arriving home looking freshly showered.

They may have bought new underwear, got a new trendy haircut, started working out and doing all manner of things they wouldn't normally do, but the spouse claims they never had a clue. Many would state they didn't really want to know or couldn't face the facts. The truth is, most likely they were going through life in an unconscious state. What's great about becoming conscious is that once you master this awareness, life gets much easier. You can see more clearly how any given action will play out and whether the outcome will be beneficial or destructive. You become an expert at being fully present. How can everyone become more conscious? First you need to really get to know yourself and your behaviours. You do this by watching yourself over time. If you just start to watch yourself with curiosity and no judgment, you will notice all kinds of traits and beliefs about yourself you previously weren't aware of.

Bill Harris, of Centerpointe fame, calls this exercise, "Adopting the posture of the witness." The theory, which I subscribe to, is that you can't consciously do anything that's not in your best interest. You can, however, do them unconsciously, which is to your detriment. Now, I don't mean being aware in an intellectual way as in what you learn in school. You may intellectually know you eat too much and don't handle certain situations well, like stress or being in large groups.

Knowing in an academic way is not the same as becoming truly conscious. For instance, I knew that I was a poor sleeper, and I was going to bed with *monkey chatter* in my head, which contributed to my sleeplessness. However, once I committed to getting really conscious about how this happened by watching myself, I discovered that I would have a stimulant of a diet soda with my evening meal and then catch up on my case notes last thing at night. It was then obvious I was contributing to the issue through external stimulation. Once I started watching myself in this conscious way, I saw what I was doing to create, or at least contribute, to the issue. I now only have water and milk after 5pm, and I do my case notes at the beginning of each day.

What I want you to do is really watch how you behave from a witness standpoint with no judgment. For instance, it's not enough to *know* you have a bad temper. You need to get conscious of your bad temper and watch how it builds, what the triggers are, and which people, circumstances and environments are more likely to see you lose it. How does it feel in your body? Does it happen more when you're tired, hungry or overwhelmed? To make real changes within yourself you have to get conscious, so that negative issues can change.

B. F. Skinner is regarded as the father of operant conditioning, which deals with operants, or intentional actions that have an effect on the surrounding environment. He proposed that the behaviour of all animals, including humans, is dictated by a simple rule, which is that if our behaviour rewards us we repeat it, and if it doesn't, we don't. Make it your goal to become conscious, so you can know what behaviours reward you and those that don't, and make conscious choices about how you act in the future.

BECOME A FORTUNE TELLER

> **"Insanity is doing the same thing over and over again and expecting different results"**

ALBERT EINSTEIN

Playing fortune teller is a good start on the road to getting conscious and witnessing all kinds of behaviours that aren't serving you. If you think about your relationship, you should be able to identify predictable patterns. You know what you're doing and have done, and you know what your partner does and has done.

Most people have a good idea about what their *stuff* is, meaning the behaviours they need to work on. In fact, you could write a thesis on the subject in the academic sense. But once you raise yourself to a level of consciousness, you get clarity about your stuff, and it isn't so dormant in your life anymore. If you consciously think about your arguments, what precedes them and how they always play out, you will most likely be able to accurately predict how an argument will go. You don't need a fortune teller. You've been there a thousand times. You have the information. If only you would use it.

Consider the following equation: E+R=O. This stands for **E**vent plus **R**eaction equals the **O**utcome.

This means if you want a better outcome, you need to consciously change the way you react to an event. The best predictor of future behaviour is past behaviour. For instance, let's say you already know that when you're trying to express displeasure about a situation that upsets you, your partner won't let you finish what you're trying to say and talks over you. Then you react by getting your back up and crying and shouting over your partner, before the inevitable time-worn outcome of someone walking out. At this point, maybe you should consider a different reaction to what upsets you. I'm asking you to *try* something different. For instance:

1. Put your hand up as a stop sign and tell your partner to please let you finish and to keep their voice down. If they keep up the undesired behaviour, remove yourself and say you'll return and talk when everything is calm.

2. Don't react in the moment. Take some time to think about what the event means to you, what it is about the event you would like to resolve and what outcome you're looking for. Then ask for a calm discussion.

3. If these don't work, ask to see a marriage counsellor to help with communication issues.

It takes two to tango, so decide you won't continue to engage in a toxic dance that's a negative behavioural loop you've seen play out time and time again. And with better accuracy than a fortune teller, you know how it will end. Hit the reset button and try again. If the new technique fails, try something else and adopt the frame of mind that you never really fail, you only get feedback about what doesn't work.

FORGIVE IT OR FORGET IT

> **"Out beyond notions of right and wrong is a field. Meet me there."**
>
> RUMI

Whether your relationship is recovering from an affair, financial infidelity, resentments, family issues, social problems or a dysfunction of any kind, there needs to be the capacity to forgive. If you truly want your relationship to not only survive but improve in every way, each of you needs to forgive the past and put it to rest forever.

Many people make excuses to avoid the work involved in fixing relationship issues. They say things like, "That's just the way he is" or maybe, "She always finds a way to spend our money." Failing to forgive can mean room is never made for the possibility that your partner can turn negative behaviours around. The truth is, many times they can. You just have to create the right conditions for success.

One of the goals for successful relationship repair is the same as the goal for mediation, which is for both parties to move away from *right fighting* and holding on for dear life to a *You're the problem* position and instead move towards fair, gainful and equitable outcomes for both parties. The old adage of, *Would you rather be right or be happy?* is applicable here. I'm not saying to forget the affair, the lies or the trespasses, but I am saying that if you want to save the relationship and move on, you're going to have to decide to put the ill will in the past and create a clean slate in order to build a new relationship landscape.

I'd like to address guilt turned inwards. If you're the transgressor and don't believe you're worthy of forgiveness, you're going to have to change your mind about that. To have any hope of having a fair and equitable relationship to invest your life into, you need to understand you can't keep saying sorry forever. The truth is that everyone makes mistakes, but the idea is to learn from them rather than stay in torturous guilt. While guilt can be a worthwhile emotion, because it alerts your sensibilities to what you're doing wrong to others, it will mean suffering and disappointment for you. When it comes to relationships, if you decide to wallow in guilt, be depressed and not like yourself, your significant other can get caught in your cycle of negativity and suffer right along with you.

Guilt can come out in isolating ways. You may withdraw and be more critical of yourself and others, and this affects everyone in the household, including the pets. In order to have good self-esteem and love yourself, you have to accept that you're human with human failings. So if you've transgressed, make peace with the transgression and yourself with a commitment to learn from your mistakes and become a better person, rather than getting stuck in a negative loop of the past.

> "The weak can never forgive. Forgiveness
> is the attribute of the strong."

MAHATMA GANDHI,
All Men are Brothers: Autobiographical Reflection

If you continue to let the same issues infiltrate the relationship due to dragging the past into the future over and over again, it's unlikely the relationship will recover. You need to bury and put a headstone on the past and create a new and more positive history. One that's created under the new policy and procedures agreed to by both of you, so the relationship can start growing in the right direction.

It's important for couples to see their relationship as a blossoming one, it's just that the same two people are in it. I ask clients to try and move through past hurts and not let old grievances have breath in their new future. To soften their hearts and minds, so they can allow for the possibility their partner has the ability to change in the ways needed to generate healing. If one partner doesn't believe and can't wait to pounce on the other the second they backslide or make a mistake, they're creating an environment conducive to failure.

STOP SPREADING THE NEWS

There's a real need for confidentiality in a relationship. No one should know what's going on in a relationship other than the people involved in it. If there's been an affair, or any other kind of major transgression against one party, and they've told their parents, their siblings, their friends and co-workers, it can absolutely change the way the transgressor is seen by significant others and alter relationships forever.

Imagine family dinners, social engagements with friends and work functions and how uncomfortable they'll be after they've heard how bad, untrustworthy and irresponsible your partner has been. They may even make high and mighty judgments about you for staying in the relationship and think you're spineless and stupid for putting up with your partner's transgressions. In the end, they may decide you can't manage your own life.

You can see how downloading your issues with the wrong people can make moving forward that much more difficult. Of course, outsiders have no right to judge you or your situation, but the reality is that they will, which can add another whole layer to an already difficult time. So who are the right people to talk to if you need to debrief? You can talk to your counsellor, or if you can't afford one, you can ring Life Line or similar free services. You can even create an audio diary on your phone and talk to yourself or journal your feelings as a way of processing and understanding your emotions. These kinds of self-debriefing activities can often be a great way to come to your own realisations, or get conscious about what's *really* going on. It can motivate you to bring about positive change.

Let me be perfectly clear. I'm not talking about domestic violence. If you need rescuing, it's absolutely fair to call everyone you know, including the police and fire brigade. What I'm talking about is controlling gossip and social media around the issues that have caused the relationship breakdown. I can't tell you the amount of times I've worked successfully with couples and gotten their relationships well on the way to recovery, with both partners doing really well, when all of that hard work is shot to hell because someone in the family or social circle brings up issues from the past.

For example, a couple may have worked hard to recover from one of the partners engaging in a one-night stand. Years have passed, and for all intents and purposes they have a new and happy marriage. Then one day at a family barbecue, a drunken relative says something like, "So, is she still screwing around on you?" This is a good example of how talking about private issues to others can drag the past into the present and cause great upset. In some cases, it causes irreversible damage. My advice is to debrief with your therapist and not your mother.

DON'T BELIEVE THE EVIDENCE

> **"In fact, all beliefs are true in the sense that all beliefs generate their own evidence."**
>
> BILL HARRIS.

Human beings have the uncanny ability to find evidence to support their beliefs and filter out evidence that doesn't support them. The brain is like a target-seeking missile. The minute you tell it to believe something, it goes about the business of seeking out evidence to prove it. The brain won't wonder if your belief is faulty or not. It will just do as you instructed to help you prove you're right about that belief.

You may spend a great deal of energy trying to figure out what causes your partner's negative behaviours and come up with all kinds of theories as to why. All the while you're forming a whole narrative in your head as to what they're thinking and feeling. I've discovered there are a few ways this happens. One way is to hold a certain belief subconsciously, consciously or both, and attract people and events, or be attracted to people and events, that confirm the belief.

For instance, if you believe no one at work likes you, then you will find all kinds of evidence to support this and filter out all evidence to dispute it. A colleague might walk past your desk and not say hello to you, and you see this as evidence he doesn't value or like you, while failing to notice he also walked by everyone else's desk and didn't offer them a greeting.

A woman may feel her husband is ashamed of her weight and is not proud of her. She's gathered evidence to support this belief, like how he never asks her to his work Christmas parties, and he never brings colleagues over to the house. He also doesn't take her out to dinner where they can be seen together in a nice, perhaps even romantic, setting. However, she filters out all of the other evidence to dispute this belief. For example, Christmas parties may be for employees only, and he doesn't ask colleagues over for dinner because he hates their guts. He may also never organise a night out, because he's a penny pincher, and the idea that his wife feels he's not proud of her would be abhorrent to him.

I've had countless clients who just decide what their partner is thinking and feeling, and ultimately have been way off the mark. For instance, a man may claim that his wife doesn't show him love, because she never cooks the Italian food she knows he loves and never wants to go to food festivals or wine and cheese nights with him anymore. The truth is that she loves him but knows he needs to watch his cholesterol and weight and doesn't want him to get ill or die from such a high-fat diet. She doesn't tell him why, because she knows he's sensitive about his weight gain and doesn't want to call attention to it.

People caught in situations like these may believe all kinds of untrue scenarios, because *they have the evidence!*

Another example is when someone moulds and contorts events to line up with their belief. So in any given neutral scenario, such as not being invited to a colleague's wedding, is interpreted to mean they're not liked or are being ostracised, when there would be no reason to think a colleague would have to make room at a wedding for work associates, and no one else was invited. It's important to look at your interpretation of people, behaviours and events and play devil's advocate with your concerns. You need to adopt the skill of a debater and look at both the evidence to support, as well as the evidence to dispute, a belief. I'm in no way telling you to ignore behaviours or events but rather to look at them in a non-biased fashion.

Filtering out evidence that doesn't support a belief is only one of the ways to back it up. Let's go back to the scenario where the person thinks no one at work likes them. Some people will believe this to the extent they'll *act* in a way to make the belief come true. For instance, they might isolate themselves, treat others with suspicion, become invisible at meetings, always exhibit an aloof *I don't care* demeanour or act defensively. They may display defensive body language, such as sitting with arms and legs crossed with a stern *Don't mess with me* persona. This becomes a self-fulfilling prophecy, because people will start to avoid and dislike this person due to their anti-social behaviours, whereas if they'd viewed this as a neutral occurrence, they may have wound up being liked and appreciated.

When you're considering how your partner might feel or what your motivations are for any given action, you should consider both positive and negative explanations, but always start with asking them what's going on. If they're not forthcoming, you should tell them you expect them to put meanings on their behaviours and not leave you to play guessing games. Knowing how your brain works in relation to only finding evidence to support a belief and filtering out evidence to dispute it, can help you evaluate people and events more appropriately and stop you from making this kind of *faulty thinking* mistake regarding your relationships.

Chapter  4

THE AUTOPSY

Chapter 4

♥

THE AUTOPSY

- What Diseases Are Making Your Relationship Sick?

- Should Your Relationship Be Taken Off Life Support?

- Your Home Should Be Your Sanctuary

- What is a Deal Breaker?

- Due Consideration

- Honesty and Transparency: Why They're Important

WHAT DISEASES ARE MAKING YOUR RELATIONSHIP SICK?

I like to describe the big issues of negative behaviours and exchanges as the "diseases" of a relationship. These diseases make the union sick, and in some cases, terminal. If you look at the root of the word disease, you'll discover *dis* means without or away from and *ease* means to be at peace and at ease with any given situation. Clearly, if a couple's love for each other is changing, and they're fighting, resentful, not enjoying each other's company, engaging in affairs and gambling, there's no *ease* in the relationship.

To decide the real issues causing distress in a relationship, there needs to be a complete autopsy. You can't hit an invisible target and fix what you don't acknowledge, so careful consideration must be given to define exactly what issues or behaviours are causing a couple to move away from each other.

Each partner must reflect on the behaviours they feel are affecting their happiness and ability to invest emotionally in their partner. By carefully and methodically looking at the upsets, arguments and factors that may be driving them, the couple can get a better picture of the health of a relationship, if it can be saved and even if in fact it *should* be saved. A relationship develops negative behaviour on both sides, with certain negative loops playing out over and over again. These loops can be anything that upsets a partner and moves them away from intimacy and feeling like one half of a supportive couple. Some examples are subtle, and not so subtle, put downs, being too tight with money, flirting, talking outside of the relationship, choosing friends and others over a spouse, jealousy, controlling behaviour or anything that causes a partner to be traumatised, upset or feel unsafe.

SHOULD YOU TAKE YOUR RELATIONSHIP OFF LIFE SUPPORT?

Most relationships will have ups and downs, and some of these can be extreme. There may be patterns that seem to swing so strongly from happy to miserable that the relationship appears to have bipolar disorder. Sometimes there's nothing but sadness, and the toxic interplay keeps getting worse. When the situation has gotten really bad, you can wind up thinking, *How much more am I expected to take? When will enough be enough?*

You might tell yourself that others have worse partners, and maybe the situation isn't that bad. Friends or well-meaning family members may say things like, "You could do worse" and "At least he doesn't hit you." There may even be guilt for considering walking out. You wind up spending more time wishing your partner was the way they were in the early days of your relationship and not as they are now.

The truth is you can't build a solid foundation with anyone if there's not enough to work with. Before you think about doing the work involved to save your relationship, you need to consider if you should persevere in the face of what can seem like constant unhappiness. There are some factors that do point to making the decision to leave. Here are some of the reasons to consider pulling the plug:

- *You don't feel safe.*

    If you don't feel safe and protected in your relationship within your own home, you should take calculated steps to move to permanent safety. If you feel you're being taken advantage of, you probably are.

- *You don't feel emotionally supported most of the time.*

  Good relationships mean mutually rewarding support, love and a strong sense of *I've got your back.* If this is not the case, you may well ask, "Why are we together?"

- *You're both experts at being nasty to each other.*

  Nasty exchanges and low blows are the communication styles of bratty children. If you and your spouse see each other as easy targets for sarcasm, put downs and snide remarks, there's little chance for a relationship recovery. If you love someone, you just don't treat them this way.

- *You no longer see your partner as an ally.*

  If you don't see your partner as someone who will stand by you through thick and thin, hold you through the tough times and celebrate with you when the good times come, then they're not your ally. Is this what you really want for the rest of your life?

- *You don't believe your partner is of good character or that they're not kind.*

  If you're not proud of your partner or think they have no integrity, honesty or honour, how can you believe they'll treat you any differently? If your partner thinks nothing of lying and stealing from others, mistreats animals or displays no compassion, you have a clear picture of what life with them would be like.

- *You feel happier on your own.*

  The idea of coupling with someone is for love and companionship. If you would rather be on your own, I would encourage you to think long and hard about why you're in a relationship with your partner. Is it that you just want to be part of a couple? Are all your friends partnered off, and you don't want to be left out? If you're happier on your own most of the time, the relationship can't be that important to you, so why fight for it?

- *Your partner doesn't respect you, and you don't respect them.*

  If you've lost respect for your partner, because they've done or said something vile or they don't respect you, the relationship has no foundation.

- *You could win the gold if there was a sport for avoiding sex and other kinds of intimacy.*

  I believe humans need skin-on-skin contact to stay bonded. If you don't want to be intimate by even holding hands or cuddling on the couch, you need to find out why. Do you have a medical issue that makes you dodge sex, or do you find your partner unappealing? Whatever the reason, this is a huge red flag.

- *You play dead.*

  You go to bed early to pretend you're asleep when your partner comes in, and/or you feel relief if they're asleep when you go to bed. Conversely, you know your partner is pretending to be asleep, and you're okay with that.

- *You don't want to be around your partner, because it's too difficult.*

  You don't like them anymore, you've fallen out of love or all of the above. In that case, you should do them, and you, a favour by pulling the plug.

- *You don't look forward to your partner coming home from work, or worse, you feel your stomach drop when you hear their car pull in the drive.*

  This is a terrible way to live. You only have one home, and if you're sharing it with someone who literally makes you sick, call it quits.

When you take a realistic look at your relationship, including what it means, what it gives you, what it costs you, as well as its overall viability, you need to assess if you're emotionally safe and stable. It's not a good idea to make decisions about your union whilst still reeling from the latest attack or argument. I advise my clients to take a time-out by going away for a short break out of the trauma to see how they feel about staying in the relationship. Talking to a counsellor, even for just one session, may allow you to get your thoughts in order and make the right decision for you and your future.

YOUR HOME SHOULD BE YOUR SANCTUARY

} **"Everything in Life is Vibration"** {

ALBERT EINSTEIN

When you consider the atmosphere in your home, it's informative to look at the vibrations your sick relationship is creating inside those walls. Further, you should look at what the word *emotion* really means. When you do this, you will see it means E + Motion, which translates as *energy* plus *motion*. So when you're angry, sad, and resentful or any other type of negative emotion, you're creating energy in motion, and these negative feelings are *moving* within your home, affecting all who live there, and not just the person you're attributing those emotions to.

I want you to bear with me here and consider how science backs up intuitions, gut feelings and experiences about negative people, places and things. Here we go.

Nothing in the universe is solid. Anything that appears solid is in fact created by a vibration. You may remember learning in school that everything is made up of atoms. These atoms are always moving, and it's the varying speed of the atom's motion that makes objects seem liquid, solid or gaseous. Sound is a vibration. So are thoughts. Many believe that everything in life, good or bad, happens because it's mirroring the body's vibration and frequencies.

Deepak Chopra has written wonderful and educational books on this topic, including *Quantum Healing* and *Molecules of Emotion*. Once you understand the energy of emotions and how they can manifest in people, places and things, including thoughts, it's like being exposed to a new frontier of healing. It's now believed that certain frequencies can not only heal, but also deflect disease.

Frequency, which is vibration, has a link to health and relationships. You could say the universe is made up of vibrating strings of energy. Through my research I've discovered that the fields of science, metaphysics and medicine all concur that certain frequencies can affect wellbeing. If you accept that all things in the natural world vibrate at different frequencies, you can understand that frequency and health are intertwined. I'm a big fan of John Assaraf, who's devoted much of his life to the study of quantum physics and how energy and thoughts affect our lives. I'm totally fascinated by Assaraf, and others like him, and I love learning about quantum psychics as it relates to the human condition.

Having a Voracious appetite to learn about the nature of the universe, and in particular string theory, I've made it a point to read about this subject. What I discovered is that many parts of the human body have a sort of a sonic fingerprint or signature, and because of this all of the different organs in the body have a different cellular sound.

If you accept that anything that appears solid is in fact created by a vibration, you realise that your home has a vibration, and you and your children will pick up on positive and negative vibrations.

When homes are full of laughter, goofing about, family time, music and time spent together, the whole home vibrates with the frequency of positivity.

Conversely, if your home is full of anger, resentment, arguments, cold shoulders and other kinds of passive-aggressive emotions and behaviours, your whole house will have a negative frequency. The vibration will cause stress, and perhaps even illness. Think about it. I'm sure you can remember a time when you entered a space and immediately felt ill at ease, heavy in the body or wanted to run away. You just knew something bad went on in the space. You could feel it but not explain it. There have been songs written about the phenomenon, such as *Good Vibrations* by the Beach Boys. There are also commonplace sayings that relate to frequencies such as, *You could cut the tension in the air with a knife, This place gives me the heebie-jeebies* and *I'm getting a bad vibe.*

It's not just environments that are able to have bad vibrations. People can also be toxic to your health. I believe, as many forward thinkers do, that you can be affected by the frequencies and vibrations of other human beings. If you're around happy and upbeat people, you will mostly likely be happy and upbeat. But if you're around negative people who are always moaning, gossiping and causing strife, you will not only catch their negative mood, you can also get physically ill. The toxic vibrations of others can be contagious. It's possible to catch a foul mood and take it home to infect your loved ones, who may have been happy before you dragged the bad frequency into the house. If you're putting out a toxic energy, friends and colleagues may dodge you by telling others, "Don't invite him/her. They're a real downer."

Likewise, nervous and edgy people can directly affect your nerves. When they're full of nervous behaviour and are always jumpy and constantly on the go, they can make the whole environment heavy with a sense of urgency and panic. Toxic personalities are damaging in many ways. If children feel negative vibrations in their home, their life can be affected academically, socially, emotionally and developmentally.

I explain all of this to illustrate how you can make yourself and your relationship toxic, and so you understand that staying together for the sake of the children under these conditions is often at cross purposes to the child's ultimate wellbeing.

> **"As your kids grow they may forget what you said, but won't forget how you made them feel."**
>
> KEVIN HEATH

In order to thrive, I believe children need to be in a happy and calm home with clear boundaries, regardless of how many parents are in it. If you can't make nice and repair your relationship, you should rescue yourself and everyone else.

WHAT IS A DEAL BREAKER?

As the name implies, a deal breaker is a behaviour that, if left unchecked, would prevent a relationship from surviving. These issues would cause you to believe that if they're not rectified, you can't see yourself staying in the relationship for another year, let alone a lifetime. I'm not talking about leaving jocks on the floor or failure to remember anniversaries. This is about abuse, apathy, disrespect, infidelity, financial irresponsibility, sarcasm or a lack of empathy, underlying nastiness and put downs. Issues that prevent you from enjoying each other's company or feeling loved and respected. When making a deal breaker contract, I ask for no more than six deal breaker nominations from each party. Any more than this could mean the relationship may need to discontinue due to incompatibility and lack of love and respect.

You may wonder why I would jump in to tackle the big issues before everything else, and here's the answer. As much as seventy percent of issues in an unhappy relationship are symptoms of the big issues. So if you resolve these, the smaller ones will often right themselves as a direct consequence. I'm sure you've heard the solution as to the best way to get big rocks, water and sand to fit into a jar. If you first put all of the big rocks in the jar so they fit how you like, you can then trickle in the sand and shake it about until it all settles nicely and causes no issue. You're then able to pour in the water, and it seamlessly goes into all of the nooks and crannies that are left and creates calm and stability. Before you know it, you've addressed all of the problems associated with the three ingredients. Of course, the big deal-breaker issues are the big rocks. The sand is the symptoms, and I see the strategies to help bring about change as the water that keeps things moving but at the same time creates calm and stability.

There are therapists who spend weeks and weeks dragging out therapy and going over all of the petty stuff, which sucks up time and eats up finances while often increasing animosity between the couple they're meant to be helping. If only they'd realise that if they begin by fixing the big issues as the causation of all of the smaller ones, there would be forward movement, and it would be far less emotionally and financially draining, as well as time efficient.

DUE CONSIDERATION

I always ask for the deal breakers to be decided over the course of several days. Behaviours that are noted for change and placement on a deal breaker contract deserve to have a great deal of thought and consideration attached to their appearance on this formal agreement.

Often, when given time to consider the dynamics and behaviours that need to change, a client will realise that where they thought they had a few deal breakers, they see that one or two of them are actually symptoms of a larger problem as I described above. Couples can more accurately outline deal breakers when given ample time to consider what the true issues are.

The added benefit of being put in a position to think long and hard about the big issues is that spending this time in consideration of the diseases makes them so much harder to sanction or ignore. You can cling to a dysfunctional relationship for dear life through fear of being on your own or because you've simply become accustomed to the hurt and dysfunction. You maybe even have thought everything was your fault, because that's what you've been hearing from your partner. This way of being in the world can be like putting on an old pair of ill-fitting shoes. They may pinch your feet, create wounds and cause long-term damage, but they're familiar. You've gotten used to living unhappily, because you want this familiarity.

This is why I ask that you start practicing consciousness. It's so you don't become a poached frog and get too comfortable with the level of dysfunction in your life. Due consideration of the deal breakers, and the recording of these truths by hand, will often show you that to be healthy and happy, you have to either fix the relationship or get out of it. This act of consideration will often reinforce the commitment needed to bring about change.

Deal breakers must be fair and equitable. I never allow any desired behavioural change to be formed into a deal breaker on a contract if it negates the rights of either partner. Certain sexual activities outside the norm are a good example of an issue you wouldn't allow on a contract, because of the following:

1. It shouldn't be a deal breaker

2. You have the right to not participate in activities and engage in behaviours that go against your free will, ethics, morals and beliefs.

While you're considering all of this, also take a good, hard look at yourself. People in an unhappy relationship will rarely take the time to think about the part they played in the relationship breakdown. Many will never hold themselves accountable in any way.

When you're considering your deal breakers, you also need to get honest with yourself regarding how you might be contributing to those behaviours you're asking your partner to change. No matter who you research, I estimate that over ninety percent of self-development gurus and behaviourist declare it all starts with you. Anyone with any emotional intelligence advises that the first step in creating change starts with you taking responsibility for yourself. All of these experts can't be wrong. Remember, you need to look at your own stuff to get clear about the problem. It can be painful to look at yourself in this naked, no-smoke-and-mirrors way, but getting clear about your part in a toxic dance is the only way to truly identify the ways you're contributing to the relationship breakdown.

If you do the groundwork on your own issues, you will be more effective at finding exactly what you need from your partner and be more willing to appreciate if and how you might be contributing to your partner's behaviours. When you look at your not-so nice traits, you can feel exposed and vulnerable, but trust me, it's the only way to change behaviours that are recurring and not in your best interests.

A common trait you'll discover when you get honest with yourself is that you're holding your current partner responsible for the trespasses of someone who came before them. For instance, constant monitoring and jealousy if you've been cheated on, holding on to every last cent if your previous partner was a drinker or a gambler or not engaging in your partner's family social occasions if your ex mother-in-law was a monster. Getting clear about yourself and taking responsibility for your part in your partner's reactions and defence responses, will put you in the best position to succeed.

HONESTY AND TRANSPARENCY: WHY THEY'RE IMPORTANT

Formulating deal breakers with complete honesty is the *key* to success. This is the time to get all of the big issues on the table and to not worry about the fallout that might come about from raising them. This is the time to worry only about being heard and getting a plan in place to facilitate change. There's no point in going through this exercise if one person is holding back for fear of making the situation worse. This may be the one and only time where both of you are fully heard, able to give clear examples and be held accountable to enable forward movement.

Honesty and transparency are vital in a relationship, because they give each of you credibility and take away any uncertainty around a million issues that can come up over a lifetime union. Many believe honesty is more important than trust. However trust, in and of itself, can be blind and based on lies and exaggerations. You may have experienced many times in your life where you trusted someone to do the right thing, and they lied to you, hurt you, stole from you or otherwise let you down. There are even sayings such as *Trust me, I'm a car salesman.* Everyone has been damaged and hurt by lies. If you find your partner out in a lie, your lives are never the same, because if you ask them a question about anything, you will never know for sure if it's the truth.

Not being honest about your feelings means that your partner has to play mind reader, and this is not a fair position for anyone in an intimate relationship. By not telling your partner how you feel about an upsetting situation, you rob them of the chance to do anything about it. This implies a kind of assumption that they wouldn't understand or take any action needed to rectify the situation. It can also put them in a situation where they're constantly trying to guess what the problems are, and this can be emotionally exhausting. It isn't fair to withhold your feelings. If there's no honesty, there can be no real trust. If you have a habit of not telling the whole story, leaving bits out, exaggerating or lying by omission, make today the day you choose to be honest with yourself and your relationship. You're on the road to starting a new chapter in your life, so with this in mind you must form your deal breakers with complete honesty.

Chapter ♡ 5

MAKING THE COMMITMENT
TO CHANGE

Chapter 5

♥

MAKING THE COMMITMENT TO CHANGE

> "**Progress is impossible without change, and those who cannot change their minds cannot change anything.**"

GEORGE BERNARD SHAW

- The Discussion

- The Negotiation

- The Contract

- Getting Your Head in the Game

- The Review

- The Tune-Up

- The Outcomes

- When You Know Better, You Do Better

When you want to achieve change, you must learn what commitment truly is. You may be sick of hearing the word commitment. You hear it in relation to your study, career and health goals. Commitment means determination and a whole-self investment. You need determination to get where you need to be. This applies to behavioural change, which can start when you look at your beliefs and what you do or don't want to happen.

Everything you've done, produced or created started with a single thought, so you need to get your head in the game to be committed to your goals. I don't just want you to get involved in this process of saving your relationship. I want you to be committed to it. Remember, the brain is a target-seeking missile, so you need to be conscious and focussed on the target. There's an old saying that goes, *The difference between being committed and getting involved is like a meal of bacon and eggs. The chicken was involved, but the pig was committed.*

In other words, you have to put all of yourself into the process. It's no good hanging around and seeing what happens. There's no room for ambiguity when trying to repair a failing relationship. You're either in it to win it, or you shouldn't bother.

THE DISCUSSION

After about a week, you both should come together with your considered deal breakers. It's important that you're both calm and ready to do the work, and there are no raw emotions or frayed nerves present from recent fighting or upsets. There needs to be a meeting of cool heads and a willingness to disengage from any toxic exchanges during this exercise.

Each person should then outline their deal breakers uninterrupted, as these are recorded as a rough draft while being discussed. As each deal breaker is described, the person asking for change provides a recent example of the deal-breaking behaviour. For instance, suppose one deal breaker for the husband is for his wife to stop taking public jabs at him regarding his weight. He would outline a recent embarrassing episode when they were out for dinner with friends, and she said, "You'll never fit into that chair, and it will probably break if you do. Ask the waiter for a substitute."

Here he's provided a clear example of the behaviour he's no longer willing to tolerate. There's no ambiguity around what he's talking about and why he considers the behaviour a deal breaker. Clear examples are important, because they ensure that the person asked to change fully understands what the problem is and exactly what the behaviour looks like, with real-life examples providing clarity.

It's important to put aside any hostility and ego-driven defensive interruptions, and to not use any form of verbal or non-verbal retorts as each partner discloses their feelings around how the other is causing them distress. That means no eye rolling, tongue clicking or exaggerated facial expressions. No sideline comments like, "Oh, sure." To do so is immature and mocks what you're trying to achieve in saving your relationship.

In the counselling room, clients often engage in right fighting, deflection and denial. It's important to hear and understand how your partner is feeling from their frame of reference, not yours. It's okay if you don't agree, but do hear your partner out. As each of you is asked to provide an example of the behaviour, clarity will be forthcoming, so be patient. There's no point in arguing the toss on any point your partner is trying to make, because they have their own perceptions and feelings, and the bottom line is that they're entitled to them. If you love your partner, you will be gracious.

THE NEGOTIATION

> **"The most important trip you may take in life is meeting people halfway."**

HENRY BOYLE

There's definitely a place for negotiation after all deal breakers have been discussed. Once you've outlined your deal breakers and your spouse/partner has done the same, the work of going through each issue to arrive at an agreed deal breaker begins. Each of you will either agree or negotiate a behaviour targeted for change.

An example of a negotiation might be that a wife has outlined a deal breaker where she wants her husband to stop prioritising soccer every Sunday and hanging out with mates over spending time with her and the family, so she asks him to give up soccer and Friday night drinks after work. A negotiation might be where he agrees to only play soccer on club days and not socially, and that he only goes to after-work drinks every second Friday.

Another example might be where a husband has outlined a deal breaker for his wife to ask her parents to give back the key to their home, as they're letting themselves in without a real reason and intruding on his privacy. She may then negotiate that she will let her parents keep the key but tell them they're to use it only in emergencies or to care for plants and pets when she and her husband are away.

In the end, there needs to be a unanimous agreement that each behavioural change is fair, equitable and clear, because once the deal breakers are outlined and the contract is signed, that's the expected code of conduct.

FORMING THE CONTRACT

This is the time to focus on the rough drafts of each deal breaker, as discussed by both parties, and make them concise and definite to ensure there are no misinterpretations or wiggle room. In a therapeutic session, the counsellor would help to shape each nominated issue into a more concise deal breaker, but there's no reason a couple with cool heads couldn't shape these into clear and direct promises on their own. For instance, a piece of dialogue regarding a deal breaker from a wife may go something like, "I want you home more. You go to the pub instead of being with us. I'm sick of you always playing sport and drinking with the boys. You need to help with the kids, and give me some down time." This is actually two deal breakers and can be worded clearly on the contract as follows:

- Must actively participate at home by helping me with the children and housework.

- Prioritise family by putting us first and only play sport every second Sunday.

Deal breakers can't be ambiguous. They must be clear and definite, so you wouldn't include a line in the contract that states, *Try to spend more time at home.* This wouldn't be effective, because the promise will have no structure or boundaries and therefore will mostly likely *not* be kept. Instead, provide clear parameters. For example:

- Come straight home from work and have a maximum of three hours of after-work drinks with mates every second Friday night.

Here is an example of a deal breaker contract to give you an idea of how to structure the behaviour changes you want in a clear and concise way that can't be misconstrued.

Date: **12/10/2015**
BEHAVIOUR TARGETED FOR CHANGE CONTRACT

Behaviour that **Cindy** requires to be changed are:	Behaviour that **Greg** requires to be changed are:

1. No more putting friends before family
  • Golf only on club days
  • Sundays with me and the kids
	1. Stop the yelling and verbal abuse. Do not scream at me or the kids ever!

2. Help out more at home
  • Bath the children every weeknight while I cook dinner.
  • Laundry – bring it in each afternoon
  • Help me clean up after dinner
	2. Stop involving the children in our fights and telling them that Daddy doesn't love them.

3. Close TAB account
  • No more gambling
  • No associating with gamblers
	3. Stop telling your parents all of our business and make and effort to be nicer to mine.

4. Do not approach me for intimacy when you have been drinking and Manage your personal hygiene
  • Shower and brush your teeth before coming to bed
	4. Stop ringing my mother about my behaviour.
	  • Leave my parents and family out of our marriage issues

5. Stand up for me when any member of your family is rude to me, puts me down or ignores me	5. Don't say your okay with me going to club matches but then act shitty when I get home • If you say you're okay, be okay
I, Greg Smith sign this contract in good faith declaring that I have given good consideration to the requested changes and I find them to be fair, reasonable and equitable. I have not been pressured or coerced in any way and hereby declare my intention to keep my promises to the best of my ability. Signature:	I, Cindy Smith sign this contract in good faith declaring that I have given good consideration to the requested changes and I find them to be fair, reasonable and equitable. I have not been pressured or coerced in any way and hereby declare my intention to keep my promises to the best of my ability. Signature:

Once the contract is completed and signed, copies are made, often by phone snapshot, so each party is in no doubt as to what's required going forward. When working with my clients I also sign the contract as a witness to formalise the agreement. However, there's no reason why a couple couldn't sign it in front of a Justice of the Peace after they've created the contract and each agreed to the expected behaviour going forward. This would add formality to the contract. A photocopy of the agreement can also be used. After a contract is agreed upon and signed, what each partner has to say to themselves is, *All I have to do is keep these few listed promises, and everything will get better. If this doesn't work, it sure as hell isn't going to be because of me.*

If both parties adopt this level of commitment, positive change will occur.

GETTING YOUR HEAD IN THE GAME

Okay, so you've just gone through the deal-breaker exercise, had the hard conversations and now have a list of behaviours you and your partner have outlined as deal breakers. You've deemed these deal breakers as fair and equitable and have signed the contract. Now you have to get your head in the game.

It's no good looking at your list of behaviours that need to change and thinking. *I'll try to do it.* You have to get proactive in making it happen. Remember, everything starts with a single thought. You're capable of great accomplishments, so make your thoughts positive and proactive. Your partner needs to see active participation on your part. They need to understand you're committed to keeping your end of the deal. If you get proactive, you will often have the effect of triggering your partner to also get their head in the game, because they can see you're doing the work.

If your partner has outlined *Stop the angry behaviour* as a deal breaker, you need to address this through a workable plan. For example, a plan to address anger might look like this:

1. Attend anger management classes.

2. Start keeping a diary on how your anger feels in your body and what caused the onset.

3. Record your triggers for outbursts in a daily journal.

4. Download workbooks on monitoring and managing anger.

5. Go to counselling for Cognitive Behavioural Therapy (CBT).

You need to do the work for you and for your partner to bring about the outcomes you want. When working on relationships, nothing says *I love you* more than putting in the work to bring about change. It speaks volumes. It says, *I want you in my life, and I will fight for you.*

Let's take another common scenario often heard in my counselling room. The deal breaker in question may be to clean up stacks of rubbish in the house and to stop being a pack rat. The plan might look like this.

1. Go to IKEA or Howard's Storage World and buy enough large, airtight containers to keep must-have items organised.

2. Hire a dumpster for one month.

3. Clear out one entire room of the house, including the garage, each consecutive Saturday until it's all done.

4. Label large boxes as *Keep*, *Donate* and *Dump*, and use them for sorting as you go.

5. Attack each room as if you you're moving or presenting the house for sale.

6. Look at the reason this habit developed in the first place. For instance, if you didn't have anything when you were a child and got so sick of going without, you can't part with anything.

7. Talk to siblings about your tendency to clutter, and find out if they've noticed why you do this or if it's a family trait. You can see that if you just put some practical thought into keeping your promises, you will dramatically increase your chances of success.

THE REVIEW

After a period of around six weeks, couples should come together with copies of the deal breakers in front of them. There needs to be a substantial amount of time to allow for everyday interactions and situations to occur frequently enough to test the deal breakers and the behavioural changes these represent. For instance, if being treated badly and suffering put downs at family gatherings has been a deal breaker targeted for extinction, there needs to have been a few family get-togethers to test whether or not this particular behaviour has indeed changed. A month to six weeks is the usual time I ask for, depending on individual circumstances. As an example, if one of the partners works in a fly-in-and-fly-out (FIFO) job and are only home two weeks of the month, this needs to be taken into consideration, and the time for review needs to be pushed out to perhaps two months or so. The idea is to review the promised behavioural changes as to whether or not they've been honoured and to what degree they've been honoured.

As previously discussed, behavioural change can take quite a long time, sometimes up to three months and beyond. However, if someone is justifiably trying, there should be demonstrated and measurable improvement. So how can you measure improvement over complete success? There's an effective strength-based tool for measuring everything from behavioural change to an emotional state, and it's called a scaling tool. This is a simple tool that measures on a scale of zero to ten.

SCALING TOOL

Circle a number between one and ten that best describes
the behavioural change around the promised deal breaker
you have noted in your partner.

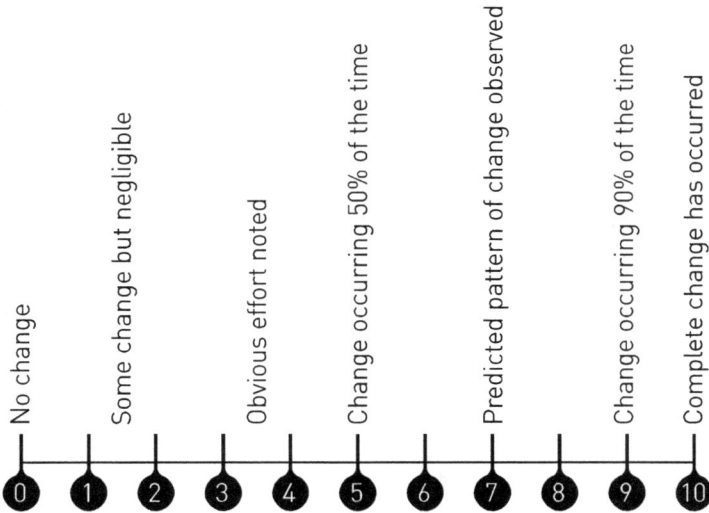

0	1	2	3	4	5	6	7	8	9	10

- 0 — No change
- 1 — Some change but negligible
- 3 — Obvious effort noted
- 4 — Change occurring 50% of the time
- 7 — Predicted pattern of change observed
- 9 — Change occurring 90% of the time
- 10 — Complete change has occurred

After six weeks, or the nominated time, you need to review the deal breakers individually. When and where you decide to do this should be chosen with the thought, *What is an ideal time to get together, and where would we be calmest and have no distractions to spend an hour measuring our progress?*

When I do this review with couples, I try to make sure the children will be away from the couple for at least an hour or so after our session concludes. When couples have this meeting on their own, they should also make sure there's plenty of calm breathing space during and after the review.

Once a time and place has been chosen, each partner sits down with their signed contract and chooses who will begin. You may decide to start with whoever is on the left-hand side of the contract. Once that's taken care of, this person will go through the deal breakers they've set for their partner and give a rating while citing solid examples of why each score is given. This is done without interruption. Then their partner does the same. In the end, the couple should be left with a clear indication of how it's going.

THE TUNE-UP

The scaling tool enables measurement of improvement on a scale from zero to ten, with a score of zero meaning absolutely no change at all. A three would indicate an attempt, and a five would indicate a fifty-percent extinction of the targeted behaviour. If there are consistent eights, nines or even tens, you're on encouraging ground. If it's all ones, twos and threes there's much more work to be done, and you have a clear idea of who's trying and who's not. High scores for five of six deal breakers and a low score for only one would indicate there's one behavioural change a partner is struggling with, and the scaling tool is effective at flushing this out and making it clear what needs to be tuned up.

In the case of a partner struggling with one particular deal breaker, perhaps it needs to be looked at more closely to see if it's as reasonable as first thought. For instance, if a promise was made to spend no more than $250 per week on running the household, but the scaling tool flushed out this was not happening, you may have to look at the expenses in detail and either find out where the budget is bleeding and cauterise it or increase the amount to more realistically reflect the true expense incurred in running the home.

It's usually at the review where one of three outcomes occurs. Not all relationships should be saved, and I believe this deal-breaker model is effective at giving the answers couples need when deciding whether or not to continue fighting for their relationship.

THE OUTCOMES

One of these three outcomes occurs if the deal-breaker model is applied.

- *Outcome one*

    The hoped-for option, and the outcome I most often see. This is where both parties change their negative behaviours and keep the promises they made in the deal breaker contract. In this case, couples go on to have a rewarding relationship that will of course still have the normal ups and downs of any relationship, but is now happy, healthy and mutually considerate.

- *Outcome two*

  This can be where the couple is able to address all of the deal breakers outlined in the contract, but all of a sudden one or both partners find more deal breakers and claim these are also making the relationship untenable. In this case, one or both parties may be consciously or subconsciously sabotaging the relationship, because deep down they don't want to save it. This usually means there was no honesty and transparency applied to the exercise in the first place.

- *Outcome three*

  Only one party does all, or most, of the work they promised under the contract, and the other has delivered little or no change. In my view, the person who didn't keep any promises made is saying loud and clear, "I don't love you enough to fix this relationship." This is important information.

  You can see that all outcomes are successful and have value, because couples get answers in a relatively short period of time, and this is information they absolutely need to know to manage their lives going forward.

WHEN YOU KNOW BETTER, YOU DO BETTER

Now the couple has vital information about what needs to change and what's expected in the future. When couples have done all of the hard work, for all intents and purposes they need to realise that even if they've been together for ten years they've created a new relationship, and it should be treated as such. When relationships are first formed they're exciting and new. Your thoughts are filled with your partner, and daydreaming is common. Sex is exciting, and all senses are fully engaged.

However, as time marches on, familiarity creates predictability, and after a while the mystery is all but gone. Life sets into formed and predictable patterns, and for some people even sex becomes a bore. Often couples will tell me they can predict with great accuracy how foreplay, if any, will be performed, and the intimacy becomes a kind of paint by numbers rote activity. *He does this and then that, and she does this and then that.* The thought of another thirty years of predictable and boring sex becomes a nightmare.

As I stated, humans need skin-on-skin contact to stay bonded. When you're intimate with your partner, you release a hormone called *oxytocin*, which is secreted by the posterior lobe of the pituitary gland and is often referred to as the cuddle hormone. Holding hands, cuddling, showering together, making love and giving massages are all good ways to get this contact and to increase bonding.

Relationships need to be fed and watered and worked on every day. Couples should stay connected by learning new skills together and growing through similar life experiences. They should also shake things up in the bedroom. I'm not talking swings and chandeliers or inviting others into the bed, or any activity both parties are not in agreement about, but rather couples should find new ways of connecting. I recommend a change of scenery, a change of approach, instigating sex on a varied timetable and trying new techniques together.

Once there's a new playing field, both parties are receptive to change and happiness is restored, it may be the perfect time to go over the pre-cohabitation checklist. Now that you know better, you can start to do better, and part of this commitment can be drawing up a mutually agreed upon set of policies and procedures. This new, extended policy should not only cover the past deal breakers but also future-proof the relationship by looking ahead. When going over the pre-cohabitation items up for consideration, couples can examine potential threats that may come up in the future and make a plan to handle them immediately.

Chapter 6

♥

THE INTERLOPERS

- Prior Relationships

- Not-So-Harmless Flirtations

- What if the Kids Are Calling the Shots?

- Setting Personal Boundaries

- Managing In-Laws and Extended Family

- Friends: Managing Each Other's Tribe

- Careers and Home Management

- Social Media

It's all well and good to decide that as a couple you will prioritise your relationship going forward and have each other's backs. However, to be effective at defending what you hope is a new relationship, you not only need a new code of conduct formulated out of the pre-cohabitation list and agreed-upon deal breakers, you also need a plan as to how you will operate as a couple against the many interlopers who can, and do, stress and threaten your relationship.

Interlopers may try to lure one of you away or cause strife between you. There are also many types of interlopers who will want to have an opinion on each, or both, of you, including how you live your lives, manage finances and careers, and how you relate to each other and raise your children. Let's look at who the most likely interlopers might be and how you can best protect your relationship from them. Brace yourself, because the list is long:

PRIOR RELATIONSHIPS

There should be no room made for ex-partners in either of your lives, unless there are shared children and parenting responsibilities. If there are children, keep the necessary contact to a minimum and only about the welfare of the children. Don't try to keep them as friends. To do so only allows them to have a living-breathing presence in your relationship. You might have heard, or know about, the new wife who has to deal with the ex-wife calling all of the time with an imagined emergency and needing her ex to come over and fix the car or the mower or some other excuse to basically mess with the new relationship. Firm lines have to be drawn regarding this behaviour, as it will absolutely affect the new relationship.

These people will use all kinds of emotional blackmail to get their ex to come over by saying things like, "These are your kids, too, and you need to make sure they can get to school and have a safe home." Here's what he needs to understand. Presumably, there's child maintenance in place, and the property division has been settled. This means he's paying what he needs to for the children, and she needs to become self-sufficient. The truth is that he's not doing her any favours by keeping her dependant on him, and he's wearing out his new love's tolerance and risking his new relationship.

Now, if you're the ex who's taking great delight in screwing with your ex's new relationship, knock it off, already. You're only achieving one of two outcomes. Either you look like a troublemaking nasty piece of work, or you seem like a needy and incompetent woman who doesn't have the emotional maturity to get on with her life. In either case, you lose.

If you have children, and your ex finds a good, ethical and nice person to pursue happiness with, you should be happy, because she or he is going to spend a great deal of time with *your* children. It's in your and your children's best interest to make sure they have a good and stable environment when they visit the non-custodial parent. If your ex doesn't choose a responsible person, you need to revisit the parenting agreement and access plan with the appropriate professionals.

Don't keep photos of your ex. If there are wedding albums and dear keepsakes, put them away out of sight, and for heaven's sake don't keep them alive on social media. Think long and hard before adding an ex to your friends list on Facebook, or any other online forum, or for that matter having any social interactions with them at all. While many therapists believe friendship with an ex can work, I'm not one of them. You may say to yourself, *But we were friends and had some great times together. We were a big part of each other's lives, and it seems a shame to just cut them off.* Yes, all of this is true, and it's the reason they need to be placed firmly in your rear-view mirror.

Think about it. If your partner has been intimate with someone, shared their life and love with them, had mutual friends, were close to each other's families, had fun adventures together, declared "I love you" to them and depended on them for emotional support, would you want them to stay in your partner's life? I'm guessing the answer is a big fat NO!

So don't ask them to accept having your ex on the scene. Trust me, it's a complication that can grow distrust and turn into the issue that ends up killing your relationship. Be sensible. Never ask your partner to do anything you wouldn't be uncomfortable with. Bringing your ex into the present is no way to respect your new partner.

NOT-SO-HARMLESS FLIRTATIONS

There are few people who promise themselves to another and never again have even a fleeting attraction towards someone else. The act of just living your life means you come into contact with lots of different and interesting people you may also find attractive. Most will simply not go there and are strong enough not to buy into the attraction to someone new. However, some may struggle to maintain the fidelity boundaries, and they may think there's nothing wrong with fantasising and having an affair in their head. After all, they reason, they're not actually planning to do anything about the attraction, so no harm no, foul. Right…?

Well, the answer is, "No, not right." Because you can, indeed, do harm even if there's no initial intent to do anything wrong. While thinking you're in control, you may start to daydream about what it would be like to be with this new person. What they might smell like, what sex would be like, and how it would feel to spend time on holidays or with their family.

It can become a sort of haunting that grows and grows, until you've crossed the line and perhaps even fallen in love. Once you get so involved, your emotional investment in the new person can be all consuming, and blocking them out of your thoughts is no longer an option. You spend your days distracted by the idea of this new person, and it isn't long before they've taken up some serious real estate in your head.

Work environments are particularly problematic. Recent decades have seen work lives become more focused on team bonding, weekend workshops, skill sharing and professional development jaunts than they ever were in the past. Companies invest thousands of dollars and thousands of hours each year on team-building activities. People are thrown together and asked to be open, friendly and to share, so it's not surprising that some colleagues become more than friends and workmates.

If you try not to think about something or someone, you tend to make the thoughts even stronger, because you have to make a visual representation in your head of the thing you want to avoid. This is easily tested. Try hard not to think about a pink panther. Go on. Don't think about a pink panther. Not easy, is it? First, you had to think about an image of a pink panther and then tell yourself not to think about it, all the while having said pink panther repeatedly in your head. So every time you tell yourself not to think about this new guy or girl, you're actually telling yourself to think about them.

You can tell this strategy isn't effective, so what will help? The best way to get an inappropriate person out of your head is to focus on your current partner. Deliberately spend time thinking about them. Why did you fall in love with him/her? Do they have a lovely face and a kind and compassionate personality? Are they funny, intelligent and dependable? It doesn't matter what trait you focus on, as long as it's a desirable trait to you. Take time to remember fun times, intimate conversations and encounters you've had with your spouse and the times they made you feel loved and supported. By consciously reinvesting emotionally in your current partner, you can starve your feelings for the new person of interest, and they'll become less important.

The next step to take is to further starve your feelings for this new person by avoiding contact with them whenever possible, particularly eye contact. You have the power to turn all of this around. If this situation should happen to you, it's within your power to decide to make the smart choice around managing your feelings and behaviour, so you can maintain a stable and loving relationship.

WHAT IF THE KIDS ARE CALLING THE SHOTS?

> "If there is anything that we wish
> to change in the child, we should
> first examine it and see whether it is
> not something that could better be
> changed in ourselves."

C.G. JUNG,
Integration of the Personality

One of the most common deal breakers I see in my work is how the children are raised and disciplined. I hear everything from, "You always put the kids first" to "It's your fault no one invites us anywhere, because the kids are wild animals." Apart from providing necessities and a loving home, the most important role of parenting is raising a child to be independent, empathetic and socially responsible. This means providing clear boundaries within which the children know they must operate.

When children have gotten out of control and consistently misbehave, the home environment becomes alive with the frequency of chaos and stress. Parents often feel at a loss as to what to do, especially when the pattern of misbehaving has been going on for some time. What most people don't realise is that a misbehaving child is often a sign they're stressed, fearful, being bullied, emotionally overwhelmed or any number of other issues they might be struggling with. The child brings negative emotions home to infect the house, which may be seen as the only safe place to lash out. These kinds of emotional issues need to be noticed and addressed.

It's more than worthwhile for parents to learn strong parenting strategies, and above all, be united in deciding rules and boundaries within the home. When parents are in control, and the child sees that someone is in charge, they tend to be calmer and do much better in all ways, including school, personal development and social skills.

Children thrive when they know there's order to their world and clear boundaries and predictability, because this makes them feel safe. If a child can cause chaos in the home, pit Mum and Dad against each other and raise Merry Hell in the home, they may feel like nobody is running the show, and this leads to fear and insecurity.

I've worked for many years as an early childhood educator, and I've seen children be mislabelled as bad, naughty, a troublemaker and even as evil. Effective parents know that first you must recognise the behaviour as being separate from the child and not identify the child as the behaviour. If you say to your child, "You're a brat," you're attacking the child. If you say, "Your behaviour is not acceptable" you're attacking the behaviour. By making this distinction, you're preserving your child's self-worth and dignity. You should next consider that you need to always notice the good behaviour as well. If you only comment on a child's negative behaviour, they may see this as the only way to get your attention.

A vital component in creating a calm and respectful child is to establish a culture of respectful behaviour and love at home. It's no good yelling at a child for using bad words or throwing things, if you've just spent the last ten minutes fighting with your partner over the bills, throwing them at your spouse and using profanities. You need to role model the behaviour you expect from your child/ren.

What a lot of parents don't seem to understand is that if you let your children run wild, do as they please and escape consequences, you're actually setting them up for a sad and lonely life. People don't like them. Other kids don't want to play with them. They don't get invited to parties. They're often avoided at all costs, and other parents may bar their kids from having anything to do with them. It's sad for these children, because they may not have been educated in acceptable behaviour, social skills or even the basic concepts of right and wrong, so they go through their childhood, or even their whole lives, not liked by most people and never understand why. All of this life-altering sadness can happen, because Mum and Dad didn't prioritise respect and boundaries in a child's formative years.

As I mentioned, I've worked with children for decades in childcare centres, special needs and behavioural support units, and of course, as a counsellor. In all of this time, I've only found one technique that works consistently, sets boundaries for all children in the household and is achievable in a relatively short amount of time. What is it?

It's the *Ask, Remind, and Consequence* Formula. For this to work, you calmly ask a child to do something, and after a few minutes if they haven't done what you've asked, you give them a calm reminder. If after a few more minutes they haven't done what you've asked, you apply a consequence they care about. No discussion, no getting down to the child's level and letting them argue like a little bush lawyer. They get the consequence.

Now, remember, I emphasised the word *calm*. If you raise your voice, get upset and engage in fighting, you've lost! And also it has to be *a consequence they care about*. If you send a child to their room where they have all kinds of cool stuff, then it's not a consequence they would care about, is it?

You know your children, and you know what they value, so make the consequence equal to the crime. If they don't put their toys away after the reminder, the consequence may be that you don't let them see their favourite TV show. If they engage in bullying another child, then the consequence may be no footy for a month. There will be lots of misbehaviours between these two extremes, and you will have to figure out an appropriate consequence for each. I've found the Ask, Remind, Consequence way of discipline can turn an absolutely nightmarish, chaotic home around in just a few weeks.

There are a couple of critical concepts you must understand and uphold. Firstly, you and your partner must be united in this method and never let the children play one of you against the other. Decide ahead of time what you both think are fair and reasonable consequences for a multitude of behaviours. This only takes an hour or so and is more than worth the time investment.

Never challenge, question each other or fight in front of the children, and never fail to give a consequence. I don't' care if you've just finished a twelve-hour shift, are exhausted, have a smacking migraine or a killer flu. You must never fail to give a consequence. Before long, children learn there's no way to get around the boundaries set by their parents. There's no way over it, under it or way to escape it. They learn they no longer have the ability to distract from it or wear you down, and so predictably they change their behaviours. You invest a few weeks or months of relentless reinforcement, and the ensuing upset that will erupt as the kids employ all of the tricks they've used before and eventually learn don't work anymore. They'll bleat and moan and scream and throw tantrums as they try to reinstate the old way of doing things. However, if you stay strong, consistent and undivided, you will gain a lifetime of control and an ordered, calm home.

Remember the rabbit that has been raised to press a lever to get a pellet to drop? The rabbit will keep pressing that lever long after the pellets have all gone but eventually will learn the lever doesn't work anymore. Likewise, your children will try all of the old tricks that used to work until they learn there's just no payoff anymore, and you both need to be resilient until this inevitably happens.

I believe you will find this the most worthwhile parenting endeavour in which you will ever engage. Calm will eventually come and you, just like the children, will learn new ways of operating. You too need to be more positively engaged with your kids. When your child walks into the room, light up your face, and smile with your heart in acknowledgement of their presence. In this way you will be telling them you love them without uttering a single word.

Manners are important, but never make an upset child wait to talk to you until you watch the end of your favourite show, send an email, check that post or read the last part of a magazine article. You can get caught up on anything you miss out on during the time when you need to give your child attention, but the moment you make your child feel like a bother, not good enough or unworthy, can never be taken back. As a therapist, I see lifelong damage inflicted, due to dismissive parents.

Tell your kids that nothing is so difficult you won't help them get through it, no matter *what* it is. Tell them that family is a team, and you work together to celebrate and overcome. Goof about with your kids, play with them, dance and do art with them. Expect them to be messy and inquisitive, and don't cultivate a boss/employee hierarchy in your home. Cuddle in front of TV. Sing silly songs from their favourite shows, and ask them about what makes them happy.

As children get a bit older, go on interesting outings like to museums, plays or the movies. When they're old enough, have interesting and educational conversations about their interests. Children will always remember these times together. Tell them often they're special, unique and beautiful. When you put your kids to bed, always ask, "What's the best thing that happened to you today?" and "What's the worst thing that happened to you today?" In this way they'll know you're invested in them and are engaged in their lives, and you will almost certainly be the first to know when problems arise, such as bullying or peer pressure.

Above all, start creating this culture of calm and respect in your home regardless of how bad the situation has gotten, because it can always be turned around through persistence and being consistently predictable in maintaining boundaries. When it comes to children and parenting, you will make mistakes and wish you had a *do over* at times, but what you can do is make the right parenting behaviours outshine the wrong ones. Once you set boundaries and instil calm and predictability in the house, you're well placed to build on their self-esteem and invest in your relationship with your partner.

Many of you will not be in your first marriage or long-term relationship. Sometimes if you form a relationship with someone who has children, it can be rough going.

- **Young stepchildren**

Younger stepchildren may still be coming to terms with the family fracture and resent your presence. They may see you as a barrier to their parents reuniting and cart tales from one household to the next, taking on the role of spy for one parent. They might also play one parent against the other and be unruly and hard to manage.

The biological parent may be guilt ridden about putting the kids through the separation and buy them all sorts of unnecessary and undeserved gifts, while also letting them get away with murder rather than upset them. In the case of younger stepchildren, I strongly advise using the Ask, Remind Consequence structure, and making sure you and your partner are on the same page. If you're united in expectations around respect and behaviour, the children will soon learn they have to at least be polite and considerate in your home.

Remember, they may be confused, angry and suffering emotional trauma. The trauma may also coincide with the normal developmental upheavals such as puberty and social pressures. Treat your stepchildren well, and make sure they feel wanted and cared for in your environment.

When it comes to finances around children not biologically yours, it's important to not make this your focus. If there are expenses around the stepchildren that are not taken care of by child maintenance payments, I suggest you see the expense as just another household bill. If you get resentful of this extra expense and make it known to everyone, it can cause irreparable damage to your relationships all-round, but most significantly with your partner.

- **Adult stepchildren**

It can go smoothly, with your adult stepchildren welcoming you into their lives, but it often doesn't go so well. Adult stepchildren may doubt your intentions or have an opinion as to why you're with their father or mother, especially if they're financially well off.

You may feel judged and excluded from family gatherings and have to endure endless comparisons to their other parent. Common comparisons are around attractiveness, wealth or success, education and social standing. If you want to avoid letting adult stepchildren wreck your relationship, think twice before *going to the mattresses* with them.

Conversely, don't let them disrespect you in any way. You need to have your partner's support in this and find that line where you don't give them fuel to fire up their campaign to split up the relationship but also maintain respect. If you go into the relationship expecting there to be barriers and are ready to face them, you may find the going easier, and you won't be disappointed.

You might also consider that it can be devastating to see your parent with someone who makes them happy and seems to love them for who they are, warts and all. It can hurt to know that your biological parents couldn't achieve this level of loving partnership in their marriage. It's important to realise that this has nothing to do with you and everything to do with disappointment in how their family of origin has now fractured.

Imagine how it would feel if your dad was depressed, largely disengaged and unavailable when he was with your mother. You rarely saw any displays of affection, they argued all of the time, and he never genuinely laughed with his heart. Then he takes up with someone else, and he's always happy and engaged. He hugs his new wife all of the time, and they seem to always be in a deep and meaningful conversation. He's started to hug you and tell you he loves you, and you think to yourself, *Now he loves us? He's just copying her.* You can see how witnessing all of this can hurt, so tread gently.

SETTING PERSONAL BOUNDARIES

One way to foster respect from your children, and others who may have cause to stay at your house, is to claim back some personal real estate. Before you had children you had each other. If you're married you most likely declared some version of *til death do us part* and not *until your lack of parenting skills makes you hate each other*. Revisiting the idea of a calm and respectful culture within the home, you need to consider how, as a couple, you can maintain romance, private space and ways to not share everything with the children and visitors. When working with clients I always suggest a *No Go* policy for the master bedroom, the en-suite and the parents' retreat, if you're lucky enough to have one.

It's worthwhile to educate the children about privacy and personal space and not a good idea to let them treat the master bedroom like a second family room. Many times couples struggling with intimacy will tell me their kids watch TV in Mum and Dad's room, crawl into the bed with them in the morning without knocking or just hang out in there if they're out.

If you let children use your bedroom like a common area, not only are you giving away couples real estate, but the end result is that nothing is sacred. You will lose clothes, makeup, expensive shampoos and be cleaning up twice as much family mess. There will be nowhere in the house for you to just have things the way you like them or be intimate without fear of an intruder, and ultimately your relationship will suffer.

Your older children should learn that if you're lying down because you're tired or sick that they can't just come in and annoy you for any little thing they decide is important, and that they must respect your need for privacy and rest. It's good for children to understand parents aren't just mothers and fathers whose world revolves around them. You're husbands and wives, daughters and sons, and individuals with your own interests, pursuits and goals. This is positive role modelling for children.

Likewise, you should maintain your separate identity and individualism for your partner. You don't want your spouse to see you only as a mother or a dad. Remember who you were when you first met, and keep the romance alive. A good rule is to have the master bedroom off limits unless someone's invited in. If your children are older, and they're used to helping themselves to your things and invading your private rooms, tell them the situation has changed, and you're no longer giving them open slather to these areas.

If they ignore your wishes and keep trespassing, put a lock on your bedroom door with only you and your spouse having a key. Sounds extreme, I know, but it works, and I can tell you I've never had a client regret doing this. Every family needs an advocate or, as Dr Phil would say, a hero. You're reading this right now, and that tells me you're ready to at least explore change.

MANAGING IN-LAWS AND EXTENDED FAMILY

I always encourage couples to agree on firm boundaries around how relationships with in-laws will be managed. When you marry or form a de-facto relationship, ideally you create a united identity that's separate from your parents and family of origin. This new identity should make its own decisions and be free of parental and extended family interference.

This doesn't mean you can't ask for advice from elders or siblings when you need it about issues like buying a house or other non-personal matters, but you need to get your priorities and loyalties in order, especially if there's conflict between partners and parents. No matter what the fight is about, you need to support your spouse, and not your family of origin, in any conflict.

Never create an *us* (me and my family) against *them* (the spouse) playing field. As discussed, you should agree on how in-laws will be managed from the outset before there's an issue. However, if you haven't done this already, it's wise to do so now. Don't discuss personal marital issues with parents and don't make declarations or promises about anything before discussing it with your spouse. Disregarding this rule is a land mine you don't want to trip.

> "A man loves his sweetheart the
> most, his wife the best, but his
> mother the longest."

IRISH PROVERB

It's especially tricky territory when getting between a man and his mother. The mother is the first and most important female figure in his life. When he marries he has to negotiate carefully to uphold both his responsibly to have his wife as his priority and to maintain the love and respect he's developed for his mother. Just being aware of this dynamic can help couples set healthy boundaries.

Whilst it's nice your parents are concerned with your welfare and career, they should respect your marital decisions, unless there's an obvious abuse occurring where they would naturally seek to rescue their child.

It's important for each of you to manage your own parents and families of origin. If your spouse is having trouble with one or both of your parents, you should be the one to step in and manage the relationship. Remember, your partner has only been in the family a short time, and you have a lifetime of familiarity. It's you who has the primary history with your parents.

As discussed earlier in regards to not spreading the news, make sure your parents do see a balanced view of your spouse. If they only hear you gripe and complain about your spouse or only see or hear from you when there's trouble or a big blow up, then they're only getting exposure to what you may see as your partner's flaws and never hear about the positive experiences that happen regularly in your relationship. This being the case, it's easy to see how they may form biased opinions about your partner, so do bear this in mind. If they only hear the bad stuff and not the good, they have no evidence the good ever happens.

All of these concepts apply to extended family as well. Typically, you don't see as many issues from extended family as with immediate in-laws, but the guidelines are the same. Keep issues with each other between you, again, unless someone needs rescuing, and always make each other a priority. You each need to be the first call when deciding how the people in your life need to be managed. This creates a culture of trust that strengthens the relationship bond and forms a united identity.

So what can you do if in-laws become toxic? I believe that if couples have tried on numerous occasions to set appropriate boundaries through discussion, mediation and/or counselling and failed to stop the toxic interplay with in-laws, then disengagement may be the only answer. You can't choose who you're related to, but you can decide what kind of treatment you will tolerate. Remember that you're both role models for your children, and it's important for you as the parents to demonstrate on a daily basis that you require respectful treatment.

I do lots of family counselling, and it's been my experience that once a couple accepts they're in a toxic relationship with a family member and take steps to disengage, everything gets better. Health, productivity at work and relationships improve, and life is happier. I would suggest a five-point plan of attack you may like to consider employing.

1. Disengage

Don't socialise with toxic family members, and don't participate in social websites like Facebook where your movements can be tracked, or give opportunities for in-laws to leave toxic messages on chat walls.

2. Stay united

As a married couple, ideally you will have formed a united identity. Never let in-laws divide you. Why tolerate the one you love being mistreated? Form an alliance, make a fair and equitable plan and stick to it.

3. Refuse to play the victim

You teach people how to treat you, so demand respect. If respect is not forthcoming, remove yourself from the toxic person. Don't stay and expose yourself to upset of any kind. In this way you train people that if they want your family's company, they have to treat everyone well.

4. Be assertive, not aggressive

Draw boundaries around what behaviours you will accept, and be firm when backing up these choices. In this way you can protect each other from many different types of attacks.

5. Refuse to be manipulated

Often in-laws will try to get to your children when they can't get a reaction from you. If your children are old enough, let them know what you're doing and why you're circling the wagons, so they have the information they need to understand what's going on.

It's not a good idea to go into lots of details with children. Keep it simple. Let them know behaviour is an issue with the person involved, and you won't accept their rudeness. Never use children as weapons, but you're the adult here, so you have a duty to draw safe barriers around your children, even if it means protecting them from one of your grandmothers or aunties.

FRIENDS: MANAGING EACH OTHER'S TRIBE

There's no getting around the fact that your friendships will change when you get married or set up a home with someone. There are many theories on the subject of friendship and bonding. Like most theories, they have plausible and not-so-plausible components.

Here's how I see it. When you're a little kid, your criterion for friendship is pretty easy to meet. If you like jumping on the bed and catching frogs, and the kid down the road likes jumping on the bed and catching frogs, you have all of the ingredients for a successful friendship.

As you get older you tend to choose friends who share the same aspirations, have similar pastimes and who help promote a fun and mutually rewarding social life. When you move through different stages in your life you tend to surround yourself with people who are going through similar experiences.

For instance, when you get married or partnered off with someone, your single friends seemed to fall by the wayside. Many enduring, lifelong friendships have followed parallel developments such as working, marrying, travelling, having children and retiring around the same age. This kept the friendship mutually satisfying and supportive, because they're shared similar experiences that unfolded concurrently.

When you have babies, you tend to surround yourself with other young mums and dads for not only common interest and support reasons, but because your social landscape changes. It's not so easy to be spontaneous once a baby arrives. You can't be the life of the party anymore or the couple who don't mind an 11:00pm drop in. Having a baby means sticking to a schedule, trying like crazy to get some sleep anywhere you can, and the days of doing anything at the drop of a hat are mostly a thing of the past.

People who don't have little ones tend to not welcome the cries and constant care an infant requires. Invitations to dinner parties and other social events may dry up. Many couples swear black and blue the baby won't change how they live their lives and declare he/she will just have to fit in with their lifestyle. This is where you laugh your guts out when you watch them turn into dishevelled, sleep-deprived, rattled control freaks that make you take off your shoes and talk quietly, so you don't wake the baby.

It's natural, and it's right for life to change when a baby comes, but it can be isolating. If you're building a life together, you begin to plot a different course from your friends and often have a change of interests. You may become more focussed on working and saving for your first home, undertaking career advancement and trying to find a healthy work/life balance. You may be happy to stay at home watching TV or working on home improvement.

In these cases friends may become frustrated, because you're never available for nights out, and they may also become jealous of your new life and wish *they* were also planning for the future with someone special. Some of these friends may try to deliberately sabotage your relationship by *accidentally on purpose* bringing up your ex, past sexual exploits or even start to flirt with your spouse or incite fights. It's quite common for people to lose friends when they marry. You're starting a different chapter of your life, and this will change again should you have children, as well as through the natural passing of time.

It helps to understand that you change significantly, as people do every five or so years, and there are usually attitudinal changes taking place during this time that modify your interests and personality. So, you can say that you're quite a bit different now from a decade ago. Some friends change in comparable measures that trend in the same directions, but this is not always the case. Think about the old phrase, *We just grew apart.* On the whole, I believe this is quite true and apt.

I always suggest that you *never* have friends of the opposite sex away from your partner's social scene, because it often leads to affairs. You may believe this is extreme thinking, but I can tell you I've been counselling couples for years, and nine times out of ten when an affair does happen, it's with someone who was previously described as just a friend, and often that friend is a colleague.

Given that you spend around nine hours at work every day and that you're spending more waking hours in the work environment than at home, it's easy to see how familiarity can turn into intimacy. A particularly hazardous situation is where a person turns to an opposite-sex friend for support when trouble in the marriage has them looking for a shoulder to cry on. Friendly conversations often turn into personal conversations, and a friendship can deepen quickly. Again, this is another good reason to make sure you become conscious, so that you can detect where a situation will head if left unchecked, and adjust your behaviours accordingly.

CAREERS AND HOME MANAGEMENT

To protect the relationship and create the atmosphere of a home sanctuary, you need to set strong boundaries not only around your relationships with family and friends, but also around places of employment and your workload. If one person regularly brings work home, is at the computer and takes calls for most of the evening, then they're not really at home. They've just changed the workplace scenery. The family really only has possession of the body and not the mind, because it's still at work. In this case the place of employment has infiltrated the home space and crossed boundaries. Now, I understand that at times some outside-hours work is necessary. However, it should be kept to a minimum and have a definite end time. To set this boundary, I advise my clients to have an 8pm *Tools Down* rule.

If one or both of you have studied long and hard and worked solidly towards a demanding career, it's inevitable sacrifices have to be made. These sacrifices can include time away from the home, extra time-consuming study, professional development and also a leave of absence when and if there's a decision to have children. Deciding to have children means considering who will take time off to care for them, how long they stay at home and how this will impact finances and career development.

Sometimes career advancement means moving away from family and friends, with relocation happening every three years or so. This is especially true of defence and mining careers. Time should be taken to look into what the future may hold and to make choices around what is and isn't a reasonable sacrifice to make. Childbirth and illness are especially hard to undertake when isolated from family, so timing can be an important consideration around career movement.

Most couples will say that whoever earns the least money will be the one to stay home doing childcare duties, at least until the children are old enough to be put into care. However, this can lead to resentment and career sacrifices on behalf of the person taking this time off. There's also the possibility of resentment on the part of the person working long hours away from the home whilst the other gets to enjoy the baby and doesn't have to commute or put up with workplace politics. So you can understand it's important to consider all of the issues around this choice before putting plans in place.

Another big bone of contention with couples who both work fulltime is housework and home administration, like bill paying and budgeting. I suggest to my clients that they figure out who works the most hours, and then construct a fair and equitable chore chart. For instance, if one person works a twelve-hour day and has an additional hour of travel added on, and the other works an eight-hour day and is fifteen minutes from home, it's a no-brainer who should take on the lion's share of the work.

If you each work similar hours, then similar home responsibilities should be shouldered. A good example of teamwork in the home would be if one person is cooking dinner, the other could bathe the kids. While one cleans up, the other reads the children bedtime stories and puts them down for the night. Couples who get into this teamwork rhythm discover they have a far more relaxing evening and enjoy more quality couple time than those who hang out washing at 11pm and don't have a plan to manage home duties.

SOCIAL MEDIA

Relationships in the current climate of technology require even more self-monitoring and active decision-making, because as previously discussed, the social landscape has made having an affair far easier to engage in and maintain than ever before. iPads, Facebook, gaming consoles and mobile phones can be interlopers. If you're always on Facebook, playing with your phone, and engaging in online activities such as building farms and fighting wars, you're not really present. The family just have body-viewing rights.

It's common for clients to complain their partners are playing with their iPads or phones when they're watching TV together or eating dinner, and even go so far as to take their media devices to the toilet. There's no time with family or for couple alone time with this kind of tuning out, blocking and disengaging. People often spend time taking pictures of what they're doing or eating and posting them rather than being fully present and enjoying what they're posting about. It's a disengaged way of living.

I realise you can't get away from technology completely, but there needs to be healthy boundaries regarding their use. Here are a few guidelines I've set with my clients over the years regarding technology:

- No phones or gadgets at the dinner table or at the cinema.

- Phones on silent when out with friends, and no checking Facebook.

- Phones and iPads put away when watching movies, playing games and other family activities.

Of all of the social media platforms, I've discovered within my practice that Facebook is particularly problematic. It's important for couples to have boundaries around social media behaviour and understand what the potential negative fallout can be. When I take couples through pre co-habituation counselling, I ask that they make an agreement about social media before marriage, so no one is left guessing as to what is, and isn't, appropriate behaviour.

Let me get one thing clear: people who have nothing to hide, hide nothing! If your respective devices are password protected, then something is amiss. I recommend that couples agree to respect reasonable privacy but to also have a firm agreement there will be no passwords protecting their online social, banking or telephone activities.

If you see that your partner is liking all posts from one particular member of the opposite sex or gender of interest, never posts couples pictures, displays revealing photos and engages in inappropriate comment exchanges, you need to call them on it the second you see it. If your partner isn't displaying your relationship in a loud and proud way to all of their friends, never mentions you and acts like a single operator, then it's a big, red flag that should never be ignored.

Another consideration is that your partner may be uncomfortable with the amount of information disclosed on social media. They may not want their personal lives shared and not appreciate a disparaging cartoon posting about opposite genders, no matter how innocent they seem. If you want to keep your relationship strong, you will *always* and I mean *always*, respect your partner's wishes around the issue of shared information.

Stalking your partner online can be tempting if you're feeling insecure. This is another huge issue I often work with. If there are trust issues, you may play amateur detective by following your partner online and looking through all of their messages and exchanges with the intent of finding something to prove they're being unfaithful. If you've made it commonplace to track applications on your partner's phone and constantly monitor their movements, it can become a time-consuming and exhausting addiction that feels like a second job. If you're experiencing the need to spy, track and stalk your partner, you need to assess whether or not the relationship is a compatible one.

There's a simple rule, and here it is: just don't do it. If you think your partner is cheating or lying about their movements, confront them about your feelings, and if what they're saying doesn't add up, don't bury your head in the sand hoping your instincts are wrong, because there's more than a huge chance you will regret it.

Online pornography, and the fallout from this activity, is a common issue faced by couples. Watching porn online is popular, and it's so easy to obtain and hide. Pornography is perhaps one of the biggest threats to relationships, because it erodes trust, lessens self-esteem and can poison the relationship beyond repair. Whereas loving and thriving intimate relationships build strong bonds that consolidate and build resiliency in the union, pornography will do the opposite. It often objectifies men and women and can end up feeling like an unwelcome intruder who's infiltrated your home and bedroom.

Women are often dominated and denigrated, and as a general rule the focus is usually on the female participants. I've seen a great deal of men who are addicted to porn, but in my many years of private practice have not seen one woman with this issue. However, women are just as much the victim of pornography addiction as the men who seek it out and bring it into the relationship. Women tell me they can't compete with the women depicted in porn. They often have killer bodies, are young, have hair extensions and fake breasts, have never given birth and are often hairless, which further perpetrates the image of youth and can feed the schoolgirl fantasy. Women in these films are willing to do what most women are just not willing to do, and this can lead them to feel inadequate, confused and depressed.

Men who watch porn may also feel ashamed but find it's not so easy to give it up. This can cause isolation, self loathing and depression. Again, there needs to be open and transparent conversations about pornography and have it clearly identified as a deal breaker from the outset. This way no one can claim they didn't think it was a big deal, didn't see it as cheating or that it just started as something to do when bored.

If you've repaired your relationship and are both working hard to maintain boundaries, it makes sense to treat the relationship as a new one and get the boundaries set before moving forward.

Chapter  7

UNCOUPLING

Chapter 7

♥

UNCOUPLING

- Trial Separation

- Moving On

- The Trap of Only Remembering the Good Stuff

- Strategies to Recover From a Broken Heart

- Take the Lesson and Move On

- A Truth About Life

- Is There More Help?

TRIAL SEPARATION

As discussed earlier, I believe if your partner tells you they want out, they don't want to work on the relationship and are *done,* there's absolutely no point in pursuing any therapeutic model of couple's therapy. However "I don't want to work on it now" may not mean, "I don't want to work on it ever."

Sometimes a person may need some space, distance and separation from all of the fighting, drama and predictable toxic interplay that has become the relationship norm. The healthy option may be to take a time-out. If a couple has developed a way of relating to each other that's antagonistic, resentful, and toxic, a trial separation could be the unlikely saviour of the relationship.

However, if couples choose to have a time-out, it shouldn't be a short one. My reasoning for this is that sometimes the feeling of relief that comes from having some distance from the tension and fighting feels like, *I don't love that person anymore*, but given adequate time, for instance between four and six months, the nervous system can reset, and the emotional and practical barriers preventing happiness in the relationship can be more accurately assessed.

Given some breathing space, each partner may think to themselves, *I do love my spouse, but the situation has to change*. The true madness would be to get back together without a plan to modify the issues that have been driving the discord and the need to separate, because just like the movie *Groundhog Day*, these issues will predictably keep repeating until they're addressed.

If nothing changes, then nothing changes, and this is where the deal breaker model is such a great tool in resetting the ground rules, by putting the past in the past and creating a new landscape for the relationship. Having a time-out needs to have some structure around what is and what is not okay.

There are some non-negotiable rules I suggest if a couple is taking a time-out, and they're plain and basic. There should be no dating or engaging in emotional or physical intimacy with anyone else during a trial separation. No large spending or running up credit cards or other debts. No socialising or debriefing with mutual friends, and no social media reporting, fishing or attempts to make the other jealous. No participating in chat rooms, alternative reality sex or dating sites, even if you tell yourself it's just to see who/what's out there, and no substance abuse.

There will be plenty of time to make new choices if, and when, an end is called to the relationship. However, the relationship needs to be protected from infidelity and other destructive behaviours until a decision is made. It's not at all uncommon for a verdict to end a relationship wind up being based on the behaviour of a partner during a trial separation.

MOVING ON

"Lots of things can be fixed. Things can be fixed. But many times, relationships between people cannot be fixed, because they should not be fixed. You're aboard a ship setting sail, and the other person has joined the inland circus, or is boarding a different ship, and you just can't be with each other anymore. Because you shouldn't be."

C. JOYBELL C.

You've tried all of the strategies and done all of the work, but in the end you come to the truth that the healthy thing to do is end the relationship. Here are some dos and don'ts to help you get out of this with your dignity intact.

Do:

- play fair, and don't make the division of assets or other legal negotiations any harder than they need to be

- make sure you get a fair settlement, so that you're not wracked with regret and resentment, because you weren't strong enough to fight for your rights

- use all of the strategies you can to help you let go of the past and move towards a better future

- stay away from the home, workplace and regular haunts of your ex

Don't:

- develop verbal diarrhoea and blab about how bad your ex is to everyone who will listen

    - It's unbecoming behaviour and doesn't help your situation

- be that tragic person who stalks your ex on social media and hounds mutual friends for information about what they're up to

- This keeps the ex in your life, slows down recovery and wears out your poor friends

- try to lose twenty kilos, get a makeover and reinvent yourself for the sole purpose of accidentally, on purpose, running into your ex, so they'll see what they're missing

  - Sure, lose the KGs and reinvent yourself for yourself and your future life but not to mess with your ex.

- invent reasons to contact your ex

  - By using tragic excuses such as, "Well, I planned to go up to Noosa this Christmas, so I thought I should ring him and let him know, since he often goes to Noosa, and I didn't want it to be awkward if we ran into each other," who do you think you're kidding? Do you really believe your ex is going to say, "Oh, that's right. I love her and can't live without her. I'm so glad she called and reminded me of this"

- trash your ex to your children

  - Don't do this, ever! I've been working with children for around forty years, and I can tell you with great confidence that children always remember who played fair and who didn't. Memories live a long time, and as adults your children will draw their own conclusions about your past behaviour. You also need to remember that your child is biologically half the product of your ex. So if you say their mother or father is no good, bad or useless, your children will often interpret this as you saying *they're* at least half bad and useless. Children should never be involved in adult issues, so no matter what you think of your ex, just don't involve your children.

- drunk-dial your ex or drunk-post anything about them

    - You may see it as some kind of outlet, but trust me, in the cold and sober light of day you *will* regret it.

- have sex with your ex

    - It can seem like a good idea. You're familiar, there's no need to impress and it fills the gap in your sex life until someone else comes along. The truth about this situation can be different from your imagined friends-with-benefits, no-complication deal. Mostly these arrangements end in disaster, because you both might have different agendas. She may think the intimacy of sex and the skin-on-skin familiarity will make him want to reconcile, while he thinks she's providing a social service to satisfy his sexual needs until someone more suitable comes along. Intimacy can trigger old behavioural patterns and cause emotional confusion. Fight the urge, and just don't go there.

- engage in pettiness

  - You've had the fights, the upsets, the trauma and the drama, and there's no percentage in seeking revenge, trying to hurt one another or engaging in character assassination. If there's property to divide, mediations to attend or court settlements to fight for, don't be petty. I've seen couples fight an all-out war over Tupperware. Of course, the fights and conflict are never about the actual object but about hurt feelings and childish acting out. I encourage clients to take what's fair, and if they don't know what that is, to have a professional decide.

THE TRAP OF ONLY REMEMBERING THE GOOD STUFF

Regardless of who calls it quits, there can be doubt, regret and uncertainty about the decision. When relationships end you need to grieve, and this is especially true if the relationship was long standing. There seems to be a strange phenomenon, especially for women, where even if the relationship was horrific and miserable, there's a tendency to only remember the good stuff. Doing this can lead to *dumper's remorse*. You need to remember that you wouldn't have ended the relationship if you truly felt it had the potential to offer what you needed for a happy union. You ended it, because on one or many levels it was failing to make you happy. In other words, it just wasn't working.

My experience working with couples has demonstrated to me that if people can just give themselves a few months to get over the grief and emotional attachment of an ex partner, they would come out the other end relieved they waited it out until the panic and grief passed.

If you don't give yourself this time, one of two situations happens. The first is panicking and going into a tailspin. You play negative loops in your head like, *What have I done? He/she wasn't that bad all of the time. Maybe he/she will stop drinking/using drugs/being emotionally abusive or become the one for me if I give it time. What if I never find anyone else?* and so on. These negative loops seem the strongest at night and in the early-morning hours.

Another possible outcome is that the person who ended it may start to worry about the person they dumped and make a series of phone calls, text messages and emails to check if they're okay. Regarding the first scenario, you need to think about everything that made you unhappy and not what you could train yourself to live with. Sometimes when you get only a brief distance from a relationship that wasn't working, you only remember the good times and may engage in this dumper's remorse way of thinking.

However, if you make a conscious effort to remember those times you wanted to head for the hills, such as when they made nasty remarks, put you down, or any number of negative scenarios, you will realise you were right to end the relationship. When you give it a few months, you tend to remember your relationship far more clearly, warts and all, and this is why time and distance are the keys to recovery from a broken heart.

The second scenario is letting go. People have been recovering and getting over a broken relationship since the beginning of time. All you're doing by calling/texting/emailing/Facebooking to check on an ex-partner is giving them false hope. Leave them alone, so they can also recover and get on with their lives.

If you start to invest in yourself in all ways, I firmly believe you will be happier with or without a partner, but I have little doubt you will find someone to love and who will love you back. I would encourage you to take some time and make a wish list of what kind of partner you really want and one you absolutely will not get involved with. This way you have a plan in place before you run into that hot prospect with lots of flaws but you reckon could be moulded into your perfect mate. People are people, not great little real estate fixer-uppers. Look at the next person as they are and not who you'd like them to be. If there are red flags of any kind, keep on moving. As Maya Angelou said, "When someone shows you who they are, believe them the first time."

If you take a good, hard look at what was and wasn't working, and what characteristics you want in a life partner, you will have a description of what your next love should look and be like. This should stop you from taking up with the same person in a different body, as many people do. Information is power, and this information may stop you from repeating old dating habits, like going back to *Arseholes R Us* and *Women B Crazy.com* to look for your next partner.

STRATEGIES TO RECOVER FROM A BROKEN HEART

In life, few of us will escape the pain of a broken heart. Getting your heart broken is a part of living, albeit a painful one. When I read Alfred Lord Tennyson quote, "Tis better to have loved and lost than never to have loved at all" I thought to myself, *This guy has never really been shattered.* I think that it would be quite nice to rewind time and dodge the whole debacle of a love affair completely, but I can see there's fertile ground for emotional growth though enduring a broken heart, and if you have one, you may as well learn how to expedite your recovery. Here are a collection of strategies I teach to my counselling students and have used regularly myself with countless clients.

- **Cognitive pairing**

  As discussed, first there's the tendency to only remember the good parts of the relationship. Here I use a strategy called *Cognitive Pairing*. With this technique you pair a powerful negative memory with a tactile object. For instance, women often use tactile beads in various colours, each with an instantly recognisable tactile difference to each other. Some beads would have rough edges and irregular surfaces, while some would have spikes or different shapes like half moons, stars or nodules. You choose these different tactile experiences, so that when you touch them they have an instant impact on your fingertips, and you recognise which bead or object it is.

Although it might be painful, sit quietly with each individual object or bead and concentrate hard to remember every detail you can about an event, statement, abuse or thoughtless act regarding your ex. Remember when they hurt you, made you feel dismissed, let down, abused, taken for granted, embarrassed or humiliated. You need to spend some time doing this, like seven to ten minutes, just sitting with each bead or object, really feeling it and looking at it. In this way you will cognitively pair a *bad stuff* memory with the bead or object. Spend this time really imagining the event in living colour that you're attaching to the object. Remember how you felt and what happened in the finest detail you can muster.

Next make a bracelet or a long chain of some description by threading each individual bead onto the string. I've had male clients who are mechanics and boiler makers use cogs, nuts and washers to cognitively pair their negative memories and balance their view of their exes. What you use is up to you, but for the sake of explanation I'll stick with the beads.

The idea is to wear the bracelet or carry the beads in your pocket or someplace where you can easily finger them. When you start to think of your ex, which will be often in the first few weeks at least, finger the beads so that all of the thoughts you associated with each individual bead will be brought to the forefront to remind you that the relationship was far from good and why it had to end.

- **Bleed it out**

  This technique holds the belief that objects that are close, colourful and vibrant have more emotional intensity than those that are pale and distant. To practice this technique you need to think of a memory of your ex in full living, breathing colour and notice how emotional you feel. Imagine everything you can, such as their eyes, skin colour, freckles and markings or a familiar shirt or dress. Also include their movement.

  Imagine their hair stirring in the breeze and them smiling at you. Next, freeze the memory to a still-life snapshot and then bleed the colour out until the image in your head is a still black-and-white photo. A good way to do this is to imagine picking at the corner of the photo and letting the colour drain out of the hole as if it's water draining out of the bottom of a plastic bag.

  Now that the colour is completely gone, move the image of your ex away, farther and farther into the background, until it disappears completely from view. Do this several times. Again, pay attention to how you feel. The emotional intensity should be much reduced.

- **Re-frame the future**

  This technique helps a person to get over the loss of another by re-framing the future they'd imagined with their ex. You may have pictured a warm, mutually advantageous partnership with your ex that included a home, a family, holidays and a rewarding retirement. Many fall in love with the person they hope their partners can be and not with the person they really are.

The fantasy of a perfect partner and an ideal life can be so seductive that you fail to look at even the most glaring facts. This strategy works really well with the cognitive pairing strategy, because once you remind yourself of all of the negatives, you may be in a better place to re-imagine what a life with your ex would, in fact, look like.

Here I ask you to re-frame this imagined fantasy future. This time base it on the known facts of your ex, using their now-realised faults as a template. For instance, if you saw your future as mutually rewarding, having each other's backs and working towards common goals, as you remember the bad times you realise you could never communicate without a row, had no intimacy and just getting along day to day was difficult. Now you can re-frame the future more accurately as years of walking and talking on eggshells and trying to please a difficult or emotionally unavailable partner.

- **File corruption**

Memories can be painful, and there's a tendency to repeat that hurtful memory over and over in your head like a looped movie. Memories can play like this for a long time, cutting deep as you remember that painful dinner when you called it quits or the nasty words that were said. There's a strategy that can corrupt a memory, so you can take the sting out of the past and not get pulled down into excruciating emotions.

Here's how it works. Think of a painful memory, and change it one part at a time. For instance if you were in a restaurant when the relationship ended, in your mind's eye change the scene to being at the beach. The next time change your partner's clothes to a clown outfit, then give them huge, bushy eyebrows and alter what they said. For instance, if they said something like "You've let yourself go, and you're not the person I married" you could modify the script in your head to, "I've decided to become an astronaut on weekdays and a rodeo clown on the weekends, and I just can't see you washing my space suit."

This may sound ridiculous, but there's a method to the madness. Think of your memory of a painful time as a Word document. If every time you pulled up the document you edited it and changed the words around, deleted bits and added bits, pressed save and closed the document, the original would be lost forever. This is also true of memories. Once you master this technique of memory corruption, you can use it for all kinds of issues that cause painful memories, such as being bullied in the workplace. You could give the perpetrator a huge nose, shrink them down to three feet tall and give them a squeaky voice. You're only limited by your imagination.

- **Blind it out**

  This technique is based on the premise that in order to fret or feel jealousy for someone, three events must happen.

  1   You have to think of the person you're fretting about.

  2. You have to imagine someone else having them.

  3. You have to wish you still had them.

  To use the blind-it-out technique, you must stop the process at step one. As soon as you think of the person you're missing, turn their image into a black or white image, a bit like a TV set with a blank or snow screen. You're effectively pulling the blind on the thought.

  If you do this every time that you think of the person, you will stop the fretting and jealousy in its tracks. This strategy should get easier and more effective the more you practice.

- **Change the environment**

  When you begin to face life without the person you thought you had a future with, you discover there are constant reminders of them. If you don't move interstate, you will most likely pass many of the places you used to enjoy with your ex, such as coffee shops, restaurants and hotels, and these can all be powerful triggers that pull at your heart.

At home you may look at the media chair they always sat in as your mind goes off on a tangent with memories of movie nights and meals eaten on laps. You might sit at the table and notice the spot where they sat and chatted about their day and many other variants of everyday life and shared cohabitation.

I encourage people recovering from a breakup to change the furniture and *décor* in their home. Redecorate and shake up the vibe to the extent that it no longer looks anything like it did when you and your ex were a couple. Buy a new mattress and bed linen and change the orientation of your bed. Throw out anything left behind that reminds you of your ex, such as personal products like deodorant or shaving cream. Buy yourself some new luxury bath towels, and send the old ones to charity. By doing this, you're reducing the number of triggers that can keep you thinking of your ex and delaying your recovery.

- **Get out and about**

It's important not to isolate yourself and to get out and socialise. This is not for the purpose of finding someone new but to meet new people, expose yourself to new experiences and to not sit at home marinating in your heartache. You don't want to spend too much time alone ruminating about what went wrong, what could have been done and what you should have said. Wondering if they'll come crawling back and generally basking in your pain, just keeps you in the trauma longer and stops you from seeing the possibilities all around you.

- **Keep the contact minimal**

If you don't have children, cease all contact of any kind. Don't invent reasons to reach out and call your ex. If you do have children, keep the communication only about their care and welfare. If your ex doesn't want to keep the conversation about the children and uses these contact calls to abuse, moan or suck you into an argument, say something like, "Is this about the children?" If it's not, hang up. If they go off track, say something like, "Keep it about the kids, please, or I'll have to end this call" and then do it. If they become unmanageable with behaviours that are upsetting for you and the children, you might consider using a Children's Contact Service for drop offs and pickups.

If you're struggling to come to terms with the separation and are going through heartache, it's especially important to not be exposed to the heart-tugging sound of your partner's voice. A voice has an individual note and tenor, and as such can be emotionally powerful. Just hearing the timbre of their voice, that all-too-familiar tone, language structure and other nuances of their speech can evoke memories and keep you emotionally stuck. Take the high road whenever you can. If your relationship has failed and you're about to start a new and better future, there's no reason why you can't leave the relationship behind with dignity and grace.

- **Remember who you were**

  Think back to before you became one half of a couple. You were a fully functioning person with likes and dislikes, opinions and hobbies. Don't lose the true you to heartache. Make an effort to remember your life prior to this relationship, including all of the fun times spent with friends and family, holidays and activities you looked forward to. If you've had a broken heart in the past, you know you can recover, and you will most likely do it quicker this time. Remember that even though you felt devastated your heart kept beating, and you kept breathing. Sad days and nights turned into weeks, and then months, and pretty soon you were ready to move on. Take some time to remember an important person in this equation: you!

TAKE THE LESSON AND MOVE ON

I'm not going trot out the old *life is a mirror* adage, but I will say there's often great opportunity to learn much about yourself when a relationship ends. In the same way you might have looked for disease, take some time to do an in-depth autopsy on what went wrong and what part you played in the demise of the relationship. Rarely is it only one person who's at fault, even if your partner was a total brute.

Did you play some part by not respecting yourself enough to get out of the relationship in the early stages? Did you miss crucial signs that spoke to an incompatibility or that they were untrustworthy and something just wasn't right? Did you make the mistake of seeing all of the red flags but thought they would grow out of it or that you could change them? Given that we teach people how to treat us, did you teach your partner it was okay to mistreat you?

Get really honest with yourself. Did you lie, hide debts, cheat or harbour secrets? Do you have wounds from childhood that make you behave in certain ways, or did you bring leftover emotions such as distrust, jealousy or insecurity from a previous relationship into the union? Sometimes if you just spend time to reflect and get conscious of your own behavioural patterns, you can unearth a deep wound, such as trust or abandonment issues from your past. Again, it's about becoming conscious. Once you become aware of a behaviour that's no longer serving you, it usually changes. Don't miss this, or any, opportunity to learn from past mistakes.

Sometimes you have unfinished emotional business from the past that will keep rearing its ugly head until you give it the attention it's crying out for. If you do find an old scar or wound that keeps repeating in all of your relationships, get yourself off to therapy to unpack all of the information you can, identify the pathology of the issue/s and get some strategies to overcome it.

You can often learn a great deal by seeing if you can identify with an archetype. Psychologist Carl Jung came up with archetypes he drew from the observation of different, but repetitive, patterns of thoughts and behaviours that keep repeating within people, cultures and countries.

Jung's main archetypes are:

- **The Shadow**: Composed of repressed ideas, weaknesses, desires, instincts and shortcomings.

- **The Anima**: The feminine image in the male psyche. Represents the true self, rather than the image presented to the outside world.

- **The Animus**: The male image in the female psyche. Represents the true self, rather than the image presented to the outside world.

- **The Self**: Represents the unification of unconsciousness and consciousness. The creation of the self occurs through individuation, in which the various aspects of personality are integrated.

These can then be broken down into a larger list, and any person may find they have the traits of one, or many, of the archetypes.

Family archetypes:

- The father: stern, powerful, controlling

- The mother: feeding, nurturing, soothing

- The child: birth, beginnings, salvation

Story archetypes

- The hero: rescuer, champion

- The maiden: purity, desire

- The wise, old man: knowledge, guidance

- The magician: mysterious, powerful

- The earth mother: nature

- The witch or sorceress: dangerous

- The trickster: deceiving, hidden

Animal archetypes

- The faithful dog: unquestioning loyalty

- The enduring horse: never giving up

- The devious cat: self-serving

Do you recognise any of these archetypes in yourself? Are you the hero, always trying to rescue your partner, or are you a trickster who's always keeping secrets and hiding behind a mask? Are you self-serving like the devious cat, or are you unquestioningly loyal no matter what, like the faithful dog? You could find some useful information about your patterns and behaviours by simply taking a good, honest look backwards.

A solid lesson you could take from a breakup is that you can't change anyone but yourself. The truth is you don't actually have the right to change anyone, as they have free will to choose their own life path, and they also will have personality differences that make them unique. This uniqueness may mean that what you deem as a trait they need to change, others may consider lovable. It's no good marrying a giraffe and wishing they were a polar bear.

Even if you're trying to help someone who has destructive behaviours such as gambling and substance abuse, you need to understand the only behaviour you can control is your own. Many a good life has been negatively impacted in a long-term way by trying to control someone else. Think about the wife or husband of an alcoholic. They may try controlling all finances and monitoring their partner's comings and goings, whilst all the time looking for signs they've been drinking. This kind of life where you're trying to manage someone else is exhausting emotionally, financially and spiritually, and trust me when I say it's not a life a healthy person would want.

Trying to change anyone but yourself is a fool's errand, because you have absolutely no control over the situation. Whether it's trying to make someone into who you think they should be or rescuing them from themselves, it's not likely to end well. So if any of the above scenarios sound like you, take the lesson and move on.

A TRUTH ABOUT LIFE

I don't want to end this chapter about uncoupling without touching on what I consider to be the truth of life. I'm not of any particular religious persuasion, but some religious teachings can be instructional regarding life and how it unfolds.

There are four Noble Truths in Buddhism, however the one I would like you to concern yourself with is the first one, which is the truth of suffering (*dukkha*). It roughly translates to *All life is suffering*. This sounds like a depressing and hopeless statement, but it contains much wisdom.

It always amazes me how so many people think happiness is a destination rather than an experience. The nature of life is to have happiness and suffering, intermittently, for however long you're on this earth. You can't achieve complete happiness and then kick back and say, "I've arrived at happiness, and nothing can bring me down again." It's the nature of being human to have emotions that change according to whatever's going on, and it's natural for life to keep changing.

If you look at the Buddhists' view of life and their first Noble Truth, you will understand how powerful their message is. It teaches that you suffer when you're born, you suffer when you die and you suffer when you have a broken heart. You suffer as you progress through ups and downs, gifts and losses and when your body betrays you by aging. You suffer when you *don't* get what you want, and ironically, when you *do* get what you want, because all circumstances are at a place in time and time passes away.

I first experienced this in a meaningful way that I could truly understand when I was about four or five years old. My family were often low on money, and we didn't have the typical childhood of movies, day trips or holidays away. Our entertainment was cheap and easy to come by. My parents would sometimes take us for walks along the beach at night, and they were wonderful times. We would have races up the beach in the moonlight and dig in the cool sand. Dad would walk with me on his shoulders, with my sisters running ahead. We would walk a long way, and when we got to a certain point that was unlit where a sand bank seemed to reach into the sea, we would turn around and head back.

This one time I remember being so happy being with my dad and sisters. Then as we reached the turn-back point, I thought, *It's nearly over, and we'll be going home soon.* So even while I was up there on Dad's shoulders with the surf spray on my face and his warm hands wrapped around my little feet, I was beginning to suffer, because I knew it was going to end.

Fast forward all of these years, and here I am thinking about a time when my children were running on the beach at Maroochydore, playing in their cubby and running through the house and giggling. Now they're grown adults, and there are no babies I can smell on my shoulder, no kids crawling into my bed, and my father is long deceased, because it happened in another time, and those times have all passed away.

I'm sad about losing those experiences, but it's natural. So, life is fluid, and you move through it losing objects, experiences and people and gaining objects, experiences and people. Living involves suffering and loss, but it also involves happiness, and it's always and forever changing. I'm not a Buddhist, but I do believe this is indeed a noble truth, and what I want to impress upon you is that you may have lost the relationship and what it represented to you, but you will go on to have other relationships, and they might just bring more happiness than you can envision right now.

There may be children yet to be born you couldn't imagine life without. There will be great times to be had and then pass away to make room for more experiences. So turn your face towards tomorrow, and get excited about what's coming next.

IS THERE MORE HELP?

Once you learn your relationships can be helped through problem solving and applicable strategies, you may be more open to seeking help for other issues that come up in life. Where previously you've pooh-poohed the idea of counselling, you can now see real benefit in seeking help for many issues, including personal counselling, anger management and grief and loss recovery, as well as stress and anxiety management, sexual identity matters, and employment coaching. Counsellors can make a huge positive impact on your life, and I would like to tell you the right way to find a professional and ethical private counsellor.

There are a few issues to be aware of when looking for a counsellor in your area. If you ring around trying to find the cheapest one, this is a big mistake. In Australia, counselling is a largely unregulated industry, and lots of untrained and unqualified people can hang a shingle and call themselves counsellors. They may offer cheap services and are often able to do this, because they don't have the overheads that true, licensed counsellors do as a matter of course, such as professional indemnity insurance, membership to governing bodies, alumni fees, or ongoing development to keep up with current methods. These cowboys of the industry could be easily flushed out if people would only ask the right questions when seeking to make an appointment such as:

- What qualifications do you hold, and is your qualification nationally recognised under The Australian Qualifications Framework (AQF)?

- What governing body do you belong to, and have you ever been investigated due to a compliant?

- Do you carry practice insurance?

- How long have you been practicing, and what is your specialty?

- Do you undertake supervision and complete a professional development matrix each year?

Bearing all of this in mind, I would encourage you to look for a counsellor who's a professional with a sound track record rather than be guided by price. Counsellors who are ethical and have years of experience and training to draw upon can often get you positive results in far less sessions than others, so the cost can be manageable.

Qualifications should be displayed prominently for all to see. At your first session, a professional counsellor will explain your rights and responsibilities, including the limits of confidentiality and when this may be broken. They should ask you if you have any questions about them and their expertise, and these questions need to be answered before commencing the counselling process.

At this time the counsellor should have you sign a consent form and explain that it, and any notes, will be kept in a locked filing cabinet. Counsellors should offer unconditional positive regard to all clients and remain neutral about your beliefs, sexuality and all matters regarding your life choices, apart from illegal activity. There should be no bias or judgment made about you or your situation. If you feel accused, judged or lectured to, you should end the session and explain you're not comfortable with the counsellor's level of ethics and neutrality.

Knowledge is power, so do your research and find a therapist you feel you have a great rapport with and who meets all of the above criteria. There's nothing wrong with telling a counsellor you just don't feel a connection with them and that you will try another. Think about it. If you were going to a local GP, and their bedside manner was abrasive to you, or you thought they weren't thorough enough or appeared to be dismissive of your concerns, wouldn't you absolutely move your care to someone else? You should manage your counselling relationship in the same way.

About the Author

♥

PROFILE LEONIE SCHILLING

Director of Counselling and Training
North Lakes Counselling Services

Leonie is a Qualified Counsellor, Trainer, Mediator and Early Childhood Educator who's also a Justice of the Peace. Specialising in relationship counselling, personal counselling, employment coaching and grief and loss, Leonie is well-respected in her community and by her peers. In addition to her academic knowledge, Leonie brings a strong, practical hands-on experiential background to her work with couples and individuals. She's worked in both the public and private education sector for over thirty years whilst also running a thriving private practice for the last nine years.

As a qualified trainer and assessor, Leonie is currently training and assessing the Diploma of Counselling and running two-day assessment workshops to fulfil student workplace third-party practicum report criteria. She also runs workshops on how to get back into the workforce, having a healthy work/life balance, building self-esteem and handling workplace confrontation.

While working for many years in behaviour support units and special education centres, Leonie has committed a large portion of her career to facilitating learning for challenged and at-risk youths and families.

Leonie is a published author, who for the last nine years has written a weekly column in the *The Messenger* magazine, which has a huge following and a growing readership across the Moreton Bay area. It's also a popular download in the United Kingdom.

In addition to couples counselling, Leonie's private practice moves clients forward in all areas. Her specialties include couples counselling, personal counselling, life coaching, family therapy, workplace dispute resolution, employment/career counselling and employment document preparation, as well as grief and loss counselling. Leonie regularly participates in professional development and maintains a trainer and practitioner matrix.

Prior to working in a therapeutic capacity, Leonie spent over ten years as a qualified early childhood educator while upholding the fifty-two principles of accreditation. She helped children across all developmental domains in all age groups whilst assisting students to gain competencies towards childcare qualifications.

Leonie is a married mother of two and enjoys a healthy work/life balance while pursuing interests in writing, meditation, dance, professional development, and health and fitness.

FINAL WORD

My sincere hope is that you will keep this book in your home library to share with your adult children, extended family and friends, and that you dive into its chapters throughout the years as needed. Whether you're working on a sick relationship, preparing to ensure a great relationship or you're just looking to maintain the one you already have, this book is written for you.

With clear chapter and topic headings, this book can be used as an easy reference manual on many relationship topics and is an ideal tool for students of counselling.

To inquire about more tools and other useful articles, or to book a personal session, send a request by visiting my website at www.northlakescounsellingservices.com.au or by calling 07 3886 2715

NOTES

NOTES

NOTES

www.ingramcontent.com/pod-product-compliance
Lightning Source LLC
Chambersburg PA
CBHW051730020426
42333CB00014B/1245